Reading Harper Lee

Reading Harper Lee

Understanding *To Kill a Mockingbird* and *Go Set a Watchman*

Claudia Durst Johnson

GREENWOOD™

An Imprint of ABC-CLIO, LLC
Santa Barbara, California • Denver, Colorado

Copyright © 2018 by ABC-CLIO, LLC

Library of Congress Cataloging-in-Publication Data

Names: Johnson, Claudia Durst, 1938- author.
Title: Reading Harper Lee : understanding To Kill a Mockingbird and Go
 Set a Watchman / Claudia Durst Johnson.
Description: Santa Barbara, California : Greenwood, 2018. | Includes
 bibliographical references and index.
Identifiers: LCCN 2018000163 (print) | LCCN 2018001560 (ebook) |
 ISBN 9781440861284 (ebook) | ISBN 9781440861277 (acid-free paper)
Subjects: LCSH: Lee, Harper—Criticism and interpretation. | Lee, Harper. To kill
 a mockingbird. | Lee, Harper. Go set a watchman.
Classification: LCC PS3562.E353 (ebook) | LCC PS3562.E353 Z73 2018 (print) |
 DDC 813/.54—dc23
LC record available at https://lccn.loc.gov/2018000163

ISBN: 978-1-4408-6127-7 (print)
 978-1-4408-6128-4 (ebook)

22 21 20 19 18   1 2 3 4 5

This book is also available as an eBook.

Greenwood
An Imprint of ABC-CLIO, LLC

ABC-CLIO, LLC
130 Cremona Drive, P.O. Box 1911
Santa Barbara, California 93116-1911
www.abc-clio.com

This book is printed on acid-free paper ∞
Manufactured in the United States of America

Contents

Introduction

To Kill a Mockingbird is one of the most read and beloved novels in the English language. Many studies by such groups as Library of Congress have found that readers believe it to be second only to the Bible in its influence. The novel is a literary classic that follows the maturation and growing awareness of young children who are being reared in the Jim Crow South by their widowed father, who seems to be an ideal parent, with the assistance of a wise and loving African American caregiver. Over the course of the book, the children have conflicts in school and in the larger community that make them feel they do not fit in. They begin to bond instead with other outsiders, such as their neighbor Boo Radley and the black people of the community. They observe their father's heroism in defending a black man wrongly accused of rape. *Go Set a Watchman* is about a young woman's return from a sojourn in New York City to the South in the 1950s, where, again from the position of an outsider, she is shocked by the attitudes and behavior of those close to her.

Both novels are also social and historical documents that opened the eyes of many readers (even Southerners) to the racial injustices of the South in the 1930s and the 1950s. In addition, both novels throw light on cultural and social matters still relevant today.

Students will find this reference book helpful as they study Harper Lee's novels in the classroom. The book provides information about Harper Lee's life and her experiences growing up in Alabama in the 1930s. It is organized around issues that stand out in the books: race, women's status, class, the South, the figure of the hero, and censorship. It concludes with a chapter on controversies raised by the novels that resonate today.

CHAPTER ONE

Harper Lee: Life of a Writer

Nelle Harper Lee, author of *To Kill a Mockingbird* and *Go Set a Watchman*, was known to her oldest friends and family as Nelle (pronounced as one syllable) and to many of her professional friends, like Gregory Peck, as Harper. Her decision to drop "Nelle" in her writing name was her fear that it would be mispronounced as "Nellie."

Nelle Harper's Parents

Her personal story starts with her parents, whose ancestors had roots in Virginia and South Carolina but ended up in rural Alabama, in the general vicinity of Monroeville, her home town.

Her mother, Frances Cunningham Finch, who does not appear in either novel as a character, was born in 1891 and received an education at Montevallo, then a small college for women in Alabama. She had four children, and died in 1951, when Nelle Harper was 25. The consensus of opinion is Frances suffered from physical and nervous ailments for most of her life.

Atticus Finch, a main character in both novels, is clearly based on her father, Amasa Coleman Lee. (At one time a title of the manuscript of *To Kill a Mockingbird* was "Atticus.") A.C., as he was generally referred to as an adult, was born in 1880. He and Frances were married in 1910. He became a member of the bar in 1915, after having worked in the field of law for some years, though he had little interest in arguing criminal cases in court. He became a partner in a Monroeville law firm, Barnett, Bugg, and Lee, which proved to be highly successful and which his eldest daughter Alice would join as an adult. A.C. was elected to the Alabama

State Legislature in 1927 where he served until 1939. In 1929 he bought part ownership in the local newspaper, the *Monroe Journal*, for which he occasionally wrote articles. He and most of his family were very much a part of the community and members of the Methodist church, which both Nelle Harper and Alice would support all of their lives.

Childhood in Monroeville, Alabama

Nelle Harper was born in Monroeville on April 28, 1926, the youngest of four children—three girls and a boy. Alice, the oldest sibling, a lawyer until her old age, managed her famous sister's financial affairs and was her sister's mainstay. Her second sister, Louise, was a journalist and mother. The third sibling, Edwin, was trained as an engineer and was in the military before dying suddenly at age 30. From what we know of Nelle Harper as a child, she seems to have shared characteristics with Scout: she was a tomboy, a daddy's girl, and a prolific reader. Fictionalized accounts of her in Truman Capote's work and in Jack Dunphy's biography of Capote, though likely exaggerated, give some sense of her eccentricities as a child. Hers and Capote's close friendship after his publication of "A Christmas Memory" and *Other Voices, Other Rooms* would suggest that his fictionalized portrait of a spirited, active girl in those works was not far off the mark.

Capote, a significant part of her everyday life as a child, was her friend until a number of years before he died. He was also the basis for a main character, Dill, in *To Kill a Mockingbird*. Later they were involved together in a literary enterprise, *In Cold Blood*, for which he never gave her proper credit. Born in 1924, he was two years older than Nelle Harper. A child of a turbulent, dysfunctional marriage, he struggled through the divorce of his parents when he was eight. Even before the divorce, he was sent to Monroeville to live for long periods of time with his mother's cousins, Frances and Amasa's neighbors. The two childhood friends, Truman and Nelle Harper, played games, read, and went to movies together.

Like Scout in *To Kill a Mockingbird*, Nelle Harper read newspapers with her father at an early age. It is impossible to know when she first learned about the Scottsboro Boys case, but it began in northern Alabama in 1931 when she was five, was the main topic of conversation in every household at the time, and was persistently covered in the media until at least 1937 when the major papers in the country called for the release of the black men accused of rape. (In an interview in 1993, she was able to reel off significant dates in the Scottsboro saga without hesitation.) In 1933, a local case in Monroeville had similarities to the one in *To Kill a Mockingbird*:

Walter Lett, a black man, was accused of rape by a white woman, found guilty without viable evidence, and eventually died four years later in an institution for the insane. Another event in 1934, when Nelle Harper was eight, was likely to have stuck in her mind: a mob of rowdy Klansmen marched past her house to the Monroeville courthouse and was confronted by her father, Amasa.

Nelle Harper graduated from high school in 1944. Even though there are hints that she didn't particularly enjoy her classes, she developed a friendship with one of her teachers, Ida Gaillard, with whom she kept in contact until Gaillard's death. Another teacher and mentor was Gladys Watson-Burkett, who lived across the street from the Lees, was an avid gardener, and thus may have been a model for the fictional Miss Maudie.

Huntingdon College

After high school, Nelle Harper enrolled in Huntingdon College for Women in Montgomery, Alabama. She had at least one good teacher there, made some friends, and acquired a not unjust reputation as a funny and caring but unusual young woman. The school was strong in the liberal arts, but its stress on religion and its main goal to educate girls to be ladies and wives was not a good fit for Nelle Harper. Citing her two contributions to the Huntingdon literary journal, *The Prelude*, her biographer Charles Shields notes that one story, "The Nightmare," is about the hanging of a black man; and the other about a noble judge in the trial of eight black men, which resonates with Judge James E. Horton of the Scottsboro trials (80).

The University of Alabama

After her freshman year at Huntingdon, Nelle Harper transferred to the University of Alabama, living for only a year in the Chi Omega sorority house before moving into a dormitory. With the obvious encouragement of her father and Alice, her older sister who was an attorney, she pursued a journalism major with a prelaw emphasis, and wrote for the main campus student publication, the *The Crimson White*, and the humorous, satirical journal, the *Rammer Jammer*. Here she published a number of articles including some on the racism of voting laws and contemporary writers and "the Negro problem." In 1946–47, she became editor of the *Rammer Jammer*. She wrote a play for the October edition, satirizing a Southern politician who announces that "Our very lives are being threatened by the hordes of evildoers full of sin . . . SIN, between ourselves and our colored friends," and who argues for creating stricter voting requirements based on the ability to interpret the Constitution (an actual requirement for would-be voters in Alabama and other Southern states at the time). She parodies country newspapers in the February issue, one of which she calls the *Jackassonian Democrat*, which carries the logo of two white sheeted figures carrying burning crosses. She also wrote a column called "Caustic Comments."

While studying journalism and prelaw, Nelle Harper took a Shakespeare class with a professor known primarily for his writing workshops. Although some of Hudson Strode's students drew the conclusion that she was never in one of his writing classes because she "didn't make the cut," her close friend James McMillan was adamant that, after the Shakespeare class with Strode, she had no desire whatsoever to join his writing workshop. Some young writers might have been inspired by Strode, but Nelle Harper was repelled by what she perceived as his pomposity and admiration for the Confederacy. (Strode wrote a three-volume biography of Jefferson Davis, canonizing the man and the Confederate cause.)

At that time, instead of having to secure an undergraduate degree and take the LSAT before applying to law school, one could, on the basis of a good grade point average, enter law school in the junior year of college. In 1943, that is just what Nelle Harper did. She said long afterward that the only reason she went to law school was to be eligible to use the library stacks, spending so much time in libraries that the directors would often leave her in charge when they had to be absent. It is reasonable to assume that her father's and sister's careers and expectations for her had something to do with her enrollment.

Almost as soon as she enrolled, she started to come to the conclusion that law school was not for her. Biographer Shields, citing a letter from Carney Dobbs, one of her campus newspaper friends (101), and a *Washington Post* article by Winzola McLendon (November 17, 1960), writes that she "hated studying law—that was the term she used, hated." A passage in *Go Set a Watchman* about Henry's education suggests that her view of law school was less than positive: "[H]e learned little of practical value. Atticus Finch was right when he said the only good the University did Henry was let him make friends with Alabama's future politicians, demagogues, and statesmen. One began to get an inkling of what law was about only when the time came to practice it" (53).

Although law professor Jay Murphy became a friend, Nelle Harper lost all interest in law school, and 1947/48 would be her last year. A term at Oxford University would offer her a welcome reprieve and begin her lifelong passion for England. When she returned to Tuscaloosa, she did not return to law school. The way the program was set up, Nelle Harper didn't graduate from law school, nor did she receive an undergraduate degree from the University of Alabama.

The Move to New York City and Reconnection with Truman Capote

Soon after her return from England to Alabama for the fall semester, Nelle Harper made up her mind in 1949 to move to New York City and write. There she lived for a time in a tiny, cold-water flat. She worked at various jobs in the city, briefly in a bookstore but for most of the time as an airline reservation clerk, first for Eastern Airlines and then British Overseas Airways, leaving her little time to write. This would begin a 58-year residency in the city of her choice. For 40 of those years she lived on East 82nd Street.

In May of 1951, she returned to Alabama for several months when her mother became very ill and was admitted to a Selma Hospital, where she died a few months later on June 2nd.

Truman Capote had established himself on the literary scene there the year before with the publication of *Other Voices, Other Rooms.* One of his characters, the tomboyish little girl, Idabel, is based in part on his old friend. In Capote's book is the observation by one adult character that Idabel is a freak whom she has never seen in a dress. Nelle Harper is also a character in his "The Thanksgiving Visitor."

She and Capote remained friends, linked by their childhoods, but they did not move in the same circles in the city. He cultivated posh, socially prominent friends. Nelle Harper was not a party person like he was. She was embraced by a different set of friends, most important among them Joy and Michael Brown, to whom she was introduced by Truman Capote, whose mother, Nina Faulk, very much a New York socialite, partier, and Southerner, was acquainted with Michael. These successful New York City artists had an immense influence on Nelle Harper's life. Michael was a famous Broadway composer, lyricist, performer, director, and producer. Joy was an equally well-known ballerina who had been invited by George Balanchine to join the Ballet Russe de Monte Carlo. Until Nelle Harper's death on February 19, 2016, Joy remained her closest friend, even taking care of Nelle Harper after her stroke in 2007, and visiting her regularly in Alabama.

Publishing Her Novel

It was Michael Brown who introduced Nelle Harper to literary agents Annie Laurie Williams and Williams's husband, Maurice Crain. Crain convinced Nelle Harper to turn from her short stories to a novel, eventually getting an interview for her with the editors at Lippincott. There she got the attention of Tay Hohoff, who would work with her on the novel, titled *Go Set a Watchman*. The publishers' records show that a copy of *Go Set a Watchman* was "brought in by author" on January 21 and 28 of 1957, which Nelle Harper transformed over the years into *To Kill a Mockingbird*.

As Nelle Harper struggled to support herself and find time from her day job to write, she spent Christmas in 1956 with Joy and Michael Brown. The envelope given her as her Christmas present contained enough money to take off from her work for a year to write. Nelle Harper would publish the details of that day in the December 1961 *McCall's* under the title "Christmas to Me," remembering opening a card that said, "You have one year off from your job to write whatever you please. Merry Christmas." She insisted that the money should be a loan and not a gift. The Browns, in essence, made *To Kill a Mockingbird* possible.

Nelle Harper rewrote her manuscript at least three times, once getting so frustrated that she threw it out the window, only to be directed by Tay Hohoff to immediately retrieve it. She was living on the edge financially, kept alive for these last years in the 1950s by the rest of the Brown gift and a modest advance from Lippincott.

Occasionally, she returned to Monroeville, mainly to support her widowed father, sometimes renting a room where she could still work hard on her writing—but she longed to return to the city. Back home in New York, in sessions with Hohoff, she changed the title from *Atticus* to *To Kill a Mockingbird* and settled on the name she wanted as author.

The Success of *To Kill a Mockingbird*

By summer of 1959, the manuscript was in the hands of Lippincott and Nelle Harper was reviewing the galleys that winter. The book was to be officially published in July of 1960, but was delayed by book club selections from reaching the general public in bookstores until fall. *To Kill a Mockingbird* got off to a flying start with its choice by the Literary Guild, the Book-of-the-Month Club, and the Readers' Digest book clubs. It would also become a British Book Society choice and was subsequently issued in the United Kingdom by Heinemann publishers.

Sales skyrocketed in the first year of publication to hundreds of thousands. In April of 1961, Nelle Harper was awarded the Pulitzer Prize, the first woman to win it since Ellen Glasgow in 1942. By this time, sales had reached 500,000 copies and the book had been translated into ten languages. It won the Bestseller's Paperback Award for the year in 1962 and, two years after publication, it had sold two and a half million copies in hardback editions and two million paperback copies. By summer of 1962 it had enjoyed 88 weeks on the *New York Times* bestseller list.

Still, some literary reviewers were critical of the structure and point of view in the novel, some considering it a work for children. And in the South especially, complaints persisted about the depiction of the trial, the coarse language, and the unflattering portrait of Southern culture.

Nelle Harper's novel remained 98 weeks on the *New York Times* bestseller list. In 1999, a poll conducted by the *Library Journal* named it the "Best Novel of the Century." Ironically, however, it is also one of the most censored and challenged novels of the century, continuing from its publication to the 2010s (see chapter 9).

Due to her novel's success, Nelle Harper was able to afford to move into a small, rent-controlled apartment on East 82nd Street, which became her permanent home.

Truman Capote and *In Cold Blood*

In 1959, as *To Kill a Mockingbird* was being readied for publication, Nelle Harper began one of the biggest undertakings of her literary life— one for which she failed to receive the credit that was due her. By the time she moved to New York City, Truman Capote was already well known there as a fiction writer and socialite. He had worked for the *New Yorker*, published several well-received short stories in prestigious magazines, and in 1948, his first widely reviewed novel, *Other Voices, Other Rooms*, appeared. He had even sold the film rights of the novel to 20th Century–Fox.

The report of the murder of the Clutter family in Holcomb, Kansas, appeared in the *New York Times* on November 15, 1959, where it caught the attention of Truman Capote. He was drawn to the story, and asked Nelle Harper to accompany him to Kansas to look into the case. Much of what occurred then was recounted by Nelle Harper during two interviews with Claudia Johnson—in 1993 (in person) and in 2005 (by telephone), after she had seen the movie *Capote*.

Nelle Harper's cooperation was essential to the project from the first because law enforcement officials and townspeople with knowledge of the case would rarely speak to Capote, the strange, tiny little man with the high voice and fashionable clothes (including a cape). Nelle Harper, on the other hand, was a down-to-earth human being like one's sister or friend, and people would talk to her. In an interview with George Plimpton in the *New York Times Book Review*, Capote said that Nelle Harper "went on a number of interviews; she typed her own notes, and I had these and could refer to them. She was extremely helpful in the beginning when we weren't making much headway with the town's people, by making friends with the wives of the people I wanted to meet." And further, "She is a gifted woman, courageous, and with a warmth that instantly kindles most people, however suspicious or dour" (January 16, 1966).

At the end of the day, after long interviews, Truman and Nelle Harper would retreat to the Warren Hotel where they typed up their observations. Nelle Harper's notes are over one hundred typed pages. When Claudia Johnson asked Nelle Harper if she had seen any of her own words in the published book, she paused for a few moments, shrugged, and said "yes."

In 1959, Nelle Harper, especially, having made close friends with the chief detective and his family, was dining at his house with Capote when news of the arrest of suspects Perry Edward Smith and Richard ("Dick") Eugene Hickock was announced. Capote and Nelle Harper were present for the opening of the trial on March 1960, on one of several trips to Kansas.

Nelle Harper reported that she accompanied Capote on every trip to Kansas except the one he made for the execution. Even then, the condemned men wrote to her asking her please to be present, but with her traveling back and forth from New York to Alabama, she (thankfully) didn't receive the letter in time.

Nelle Harper's Reaction to the Film *Capote*

After the release of the film *Capote*, Nelle Harper provided her view of its accuracy. In the first place, she declared that the performance by Philip Seymour Hoffman was stunningly done to perfection: he *was* Capote down to the last detail. Otherwise, except for the scene of the crowds in the streets, she considered the movie total fiction.

Indeed, when law enforcement officials in Kansas heard that the filmmakers were planning to (and eventually did) show Capote bribing them for access, they asked Nelle Harper to get substantiation from the *In Cold Blood* files in the New York Public Library to prove that they had never accepted any payment. Unfortunately, though Nelle Harper made the trip to the library, her macular degeneration prevented her from finding the material the Kansans were looking for. Yes, she told Claudia Johnson, there was little doubt that Capote *tried* to bribe law enforcement officials, but they maintained their integrity.

Also important, she said, was that Capote never spoke with either of the condemned men in their cells. (Rumor had it that Capote even had sex with Perry in his cell, and the movie showed Capote having lengthy visits with him.) Nelle Harper asserted that she herself had been with Capote every time he spoke to the convicted men. Each time they were in a regular visitor's room with an armed prison guard behind them.

The other misrepresentation was Perry's confession to Capote. He had actually confessed to the authorities soon after he was arrested.

As Capote kept promising the men help with legal support and never carrying through on it, they complained of their disappointment to Nelle Harper. In her interviews with Claudia Johnson, Nelle Harper confirmed that the continuing stays of execution and appeals made Truman nervous—he just wanted to get the whole thing over with so he would be able to finish his book. She also confirmed that most people agree that he didn't really care about either one of the men, and didn't go out of his way to help them.

She (as others have corroborated) discredited the scenes of William Shawn, editor of the *New Yorker*, flying to Kansas with Capote, as is shown in the movie. Shawn was well known for his deep fear of elevators and bridges, much less airplanes. Nor did she visit Capote in Italy, as was shown in the film.

Nelle Harper gradually disengaged from the project as the executions approached. Capote, who had little to do with her since the Kansas trips, asked her to proofread the manuscript, which she did. Nelle Harper reported to Claudia Johnson that joint authorship was never intended. Before absolute proof appeared in a letter written by Capote, that he had not had even any knowledge of the writing of *To Kill a Mockingbird*, Claudia Johnson was quoted in *The Telegraph* as saying that Nelle Harper had more to do with the writing of *In Cold Blood* than Capote did with *To Kill a Mockingbird*. Nelle Harper scolded her, saying, "I wrote *To Kill a Mockingbird*, and he wrote *In Cold Blood*." Capote never made an attempt to correct the rumors about his part, or lack of it, in writing *To Kill a Mockingbird*.

Publication of *In Cold Blood*

In 1965, the serial publication of *In Cold Blood*, heavily edited by Shawn, began in the *New Yorker*. *In Cold Blood* was published in hardcover in 1966 with a dual dedication to Capote's lover, Jack Dunphy, and Harper Lee, but there is no acknowledgment whatsoever of her extensive role in researching and composing the book. Some historians have speculated that she was disappointed by this. Their friendship generally waned after the publication of *In Cold Blood*. She was invited to the highly publicized Black and White Ball Capote gave in New York City, but was not tempted to attend. Their friendship didn't turn sour because he did not acknowledge her contributions to the book, but because, for the last 12 or 15 years of his life, he "seemed hell-bent on destroying everyone who had ever loved him." She watched Capote destroy himself and others, especially Jack Dunphy (whom Nelle Harper liked and admired) with his addiction to alcohol and drugs. She wrote to Claudia Johnson at one time that maybe he wasn't Dill after all.

The Making of the Film *To Kill a Mockingbird*

By the early 1960s, with money from *To Kill a Mockingbird* pouring in, Alice Lee, her older sister, one of the first women lawyers in Alabama, who settled in her father's firm in Monroeville, became her life-long business manager.

After the publication of Nelle Harper's novel, Annie Laurie Williams (wife of Maurice Crain, Nelle Harper's literary agent) became Nelle Harper's agent for the movie rights of *To Kill a Mockingbird*. Producer Alan Pakula and director Bob Mulligan formed a company to make the film. In January of 1961, the deal was closed. Eventually Universal Studios became involved and Nelle Harper was offered the job of writing the screenplay. She declined, realizing that she did not have the experience or interest in film writing. The job fell to Horton Foote. The movie industry's interest soared when Gregory Peck enthusiastically agreed to take the part of Atticus.

Peck visited Nelle Harper in Monroeville in January of 1962, and she visited the set in Los Angeles for the first time as the production was about to begin, becoming close life-long friends with the Peck family.

The original idea of filming in Monroeville fell through when it was determined that the little town had changed dramatically since the 1930s: many of the old buildings and trees were gone; the streets were paved; in short, there was nothing of the old character left. By moving condemned houses onto the set, the look the filmmakers wanted was achieved and, by the way, at tremendous savings to the company.

Nelle Harper got to know most of the other actors. Nine-year-old Mary Badham who played Scout and 13-year-old Phillip Alford who played Jem were Birmingham, Alabama, natives, chosen for their roles after auditioning in Birmingham. Dill was played by nine-year-old John Megna. Although Phillip and John, like typical young boys, had little use at the time for their female counterpart, the dynamics of the group were overall positive, except for the actor James Anderson, playing Bob Ewell, who had a reputation for bad behavior. Brock Peters had an immense influence on the film, insisting that his role of Tom be played with upright dignity, not lapsing into shuffling stereotype.

The screenplay often changed the focus, characters, and action of the book in critical ways, although it was Nelle Harper's opinion that the final movie was the best rendition of a film from a book she had ever seen. The social message of the novel was emphasized in the film and many of the children's scenes were cut; key scenes and characters were cut, among them, Aunt Alexandra and Mrs. Dubose (first included and later cut), the missionary society, and the grade school teacher. Gregory Peck strongly suggested after the first shooting was complete in June of 1962 that the scenes focusing on Atticus and trial receive greater attention.

The film premiered in Los Angeles during the Christmas season of 1962, opening in New York City in February of 1963. Shortly before, Amasa C. Lee had died. In the spring of 1963, *To Kill a Mockingbird* was nominated for eight Academy Awards and eventually won three, best actor, best adapted screenplay, and best art direction.

Nelle Harper's Aversion to Publicity

Nelle Harper was not prepared for the press's ardent attention to her personal life. She hated it, and it continued unabated to the end of her life. She would sometimes go to Monroeville or the second houses of New York City friends where it was harder for her to be reached, and she tried to keep her Manhattan address and phone number secret. (Upon sending her address to a friend, she cautioned, "read, memorize, chew up this address and swallow it.") Her decision not to give interviews or speeches led to the mistaken and widely held idea that Nelle Harper was a recluse. She was not.

She had a wide circle of friends, chiefly in New York City, Tuscaloosa, and Monroeville. She was not much of a party-goer, but she was social, visiting with her good friends, playing cards, golfing, going to museums, concerts, plays, and ball games, and traveling. She spent much of her time in various New York City libraries. And she wrote. Despite Nelle Harper's less than satisfactory experience as a student at the University of Alabama, she made close friends in Tuscaloosa. They included Jim McMillan, John Luskin, and Doris Leapard, whom she would come up to visit when she made trips to Alabama. Luskin was her drinking buddy. McMillan, a linguist in the English Department and a founder of the university press, could offer her advice about publishing and reminisce about the old days when she was in school. Doris Leapard's great attraction was that she was an artist and from New York. In short, Nelle Harper seemed to have had a full, engaged life.

Toward the end of the century, her life was sadly altered by the deaths of friends, including Maurice Crain, a special man in her life—professionally and personally—who died in 1970 after a long illness. Nelle Harper did her best to provide help in his last days. In 1984 Capote died and, although they had long before parted ways, she attended his funeral. She, herself, became afflicted with macular degeneration, which began to take a toll on her ability to read.

To Nelle Harper's extreme dissatisfaction, Monroeville began to capitalize on her novel in the 1990s. Murals were painted on buildings, a statue of Atticus was erected near the courthouse, plays of the novel were produced, and a museum opened. Nelle Harper became extremely irate over the sale of a book titled *Calpurnia's Recipes*. When she asked that it be recalled, it was.

In October of 1993, when Claudia Johnson, then living in Tuscaloosa, was asked to write a book for Simon and Schuster's Twayne series on *To Kill a Mockingbird,* she contacted her and Nelle Harper's mutual friend, Jim McMillan, to be sure she got the biographical chronology correct. Nelle Harper remembered an incident just after she won the Pulitzer Prize when a *Life* magazine photographer was returning to New York by way of Montgomery. He got caught up in a fracas between protesters and police and was pushed through a glass storefront. In a letter written by Nelle Harper in March of 1998, she tells Johnson, who was going to Monroeville, that it was too bad she had to go to the town to accept an award but to grab it and get out of Monroeville as fast as possible—that the town had made her into a commodity (interview, New York City, March 28, 1998).

She always referred to a "Mockingbird" mural the town had painted on the side of a building as "The Next-to-the-Last Supper."

Her Firm Decision to Avoid Further Publication

Many queries and much speculation circulated about why Nelle Harper did not publish another book. She was undoubtedly working on something else not too long after *To Kill a Mockingbird* was published—a project that mysteriously disappeared in the 1970s. In the 1980s, she started on a journalistic project called "The Reverend," with a setting in Alexander City, Alabama. It involved a serial killer of at least five people, who was known but never convicted, and was finally murdered himself. She became deeply involved with it, gathering material and spending considerable time in Alexander City. She abandoned the project sometime in the late 1980s, explaining that the last straw came when a man telephoned her and offered to "sell me his grandmother" for a tidy sum of money.

There are a number of speculations about why Nelle Harper never published anything else after *To Kill a Mockingbird*. Her own explanation was that she had said all she wanted to say and, when a writer has reached a peak, as she did with her famous novel, that the rest is all downhill. She, frankly, didn't want to face the public uproar, painful attention, unavoidable comparisons, and criticism that another work would inevitably bring. She was also a perfectionist, which may have had something to do with the disappearance of the projects she was working on after *To Kill a Mockingbird*. Her involvement in the Clutter case and the Alexander City case suggest her interest and talents as a journalist and historian.

To all who were close to her, Nelle Harper insisted that she did not want to publish anything nor did she want any biography of hers published in her lifetime. She did agree, however, to the publication of the 35th anniversary edition of *To Kill a Mockingbird* in 1995. In 2001 Nelle Harper attended an Honors School conference on *To Kill a Mockingbird* at the University of Alabama.

The Unavoidable Return to Monroeville

In 2007, Nelle Harper suffered a debilitating stroke in her home in New York City. She was taken to a hospital in New York, then one in Birmingham, Alabama, and finally to an assisted living facility in Monroeville, Alabama, where her sister Alice still lived and practiced law. In the same year, she was able to attend a ceremony in Washington, DC, where she was awarded the Presidential Medal of Freedom by President George W. Bush.

Nelle Harper continued to read with the help of a magnifying screen. Her other major amusement was traveling to Atmore, Alabama, to gamble. In August of 2010, Claudia Johnson and family and friends planned to go Monroeville so that Claudia and Nelle Harper could visit. She called Claudia before the visit to report that her memory was not sharp enough anymore for another formal interview but that she would welcome as many visits as could be managed. It became apparent to all at the time that Nelle Harper was correct in saying that she could no longer remember things and several suspected that a certain amount of dementia had set in.

The Last Six Years of Her Life

The last six years in Nelle Harper's life are worthy of a three-act drama themselves. In 2011 Alice Lee suffered a severe bout of pneumonia and moved to a nursing home, different from Nelle Harper's assisted living facility. She was no longer able to fully manage Nelle Harper's financial and legal affairs. This weighty job went to a former member of Alice's office staff who had gotten her law degree from the University of Alabama.

The "Discovery" of *Go Set a Watchman*

In this same year a copy of a novel written before *Mockingbird* and rejected by Lippincott was discovered in a bank vault by two of Nelle Harper's literary consultants, her agent Sam Pinkus and a Sotheby's rare books expert, both of whom remembered her lawyer also being present on the occasion, contrary to the lawyer's own memory.

Lawsuits and Possible Dementia

On May 3, 2013, Nelle Harper's lawyer, on her behalf, sued her then literary agent, Pinkus, over theft of Nelle Harper's royalties, which he had been able to do by taking advantage of her declining health to sign papers in 2007. Claire Suddath, in an interview with Nelle Harper's lawyer, asked how a woman who could be manipulated by her agent into signing away her rights could, four years later, be competent enough to agree to a publication she had in her pre-stroke days vowed never, ever to agree to. Suddath writes that she got no answer. In October of 2013, Nelle Harper's lawyer also sued the Monroeville museum—a settlement that forced the town to make concessions regarding its murals, the museum, and the city's production of the stage play of *To Kill a Mockingbird*.

Alice Lee's Conclusions about Her Sister's Health

On November 17, 2014, Nelle Harper's sister died but not before she made clear, in writing, that Nelle Harper's dementia would lead her to sign anything put before her, including an objection to the publication of a book, *The Mockingbird Next Door*, by Marja Mills with whom both Alice and Nelle Harper had willingly cooperated. Yet Nelle Harper's lawyer produced a signed letter in which Nelle Harper expressed her objection. Alice, however, discounted the letter that her sister had signed. Marja Mills reported in the *Washington Post* on July 20 of 2015 that Alice had written her that "poor Nelle Harper can't see and can't hear and will sign anything put before her by anyone in whom she has confidence." Alice's letter ends, "I am humiliated, embarrassed, and upset about the suggestion of lack of integrity in my office. I am waiting for the other shoe to fall."

Plans to Publish and Issues of Nelle Harper's Life-Long Wishes and Present Competence

In February of 2015, less than three months after Alice's death, Nelle Harper's lawyer announced she had *just* discovered the manuscript *Go Set a Watchman* (a manuscript Nelle Harper's literary advisors said her lawyer had seen four years earlier). Joe Nocera, writing for the *New York Times*, speculated that Nelle Harper's lawyer held onto her discovery of the manuscript until Alice died, and Alice would no longer have control over Nelle Harper's affairs. According to Nelle Harper's nephew, he had read the manuscript years earlier and it was never "lost."

Her lawyer sent it to Nelle Harper's agent, Andrew Nurnberg, and HarperCollins agreed to publish the work.

Nelle Harper had indicated before her stroke that she didn't want anything else published because when you are at the top, there's only one way to go. (One thinks of Joseph Heller.) And to a friend, "I wouldn't go through the pressure and publicity I went through with *To Kill a Mockingbird* for any amount of money. . . . I have said what I wanted to say, and I will not say it again" (Butts interview). Stephen Peck, Gregory Peck's son and a friend of Nelle Harper's, was one of those who believed the publication of *Go Set a Watchman* was a bad idea that would harm the reputation of *To Kill a Mockingbird*.

The very few of Nelle Harper's friends allowed in to see her, as well as her publisher and lawyer, assured the public that she remained very bright and tremendously pleased that the old novel was to be published. But questions arose about why Nelle Harper, a notoriously private person, who had always, all her life, said she didn't want anything else published, even refused to give speeches and interviews, especially because of the public attention and scrutiny, would now, after approximately 55 years, decide to publish a novel that Tay Hohoff had said was unfit for publication. Many more people, who had seen her recently in private and public (at her sister's funeral and at an Alabama Shakespeare production) questioned her mental ability to make independent choices so at variance with her lifelong propensities.

One close friend indicated that her macular degeneration and her stroke had left her 95 percent blind, profoundly deaf, and confined to a wheelchair. He indicated that "her short-term memory is completely shot and poor in general" (Butts interview).

Her lawyer reported that Nelle Harper was crushed by the widespread expressed suspicion of her state of mind and decision-making ability, but immediately the question arose: Who *conveyed* to her these critical comments that would be so painful to her? Nelle Harper was blind and could not read them for herself.

In February of 2015, an investigation by the Alabama Securities Commission and the Department of Human Resources was launched into the possible coercion and abuse of Nelle Harper with regard to publication of *Go Set a Watchman*. By April 2, 2015, the agencies found no evidence of abuse or neglect (Kellogg, "Alabama Closes").

The Publication of *Go Set a Watchman*

Go Set a Watchman was released, largely unedited except for, according to publisher, Jonathan Burnham, "a very light copy edit" (Suddath, "What Does Harper Lee Want?"). Unfortunately, the "light edit" did not catch a critical mistake in the key passage on page 265 where the word "conscious" is used instead of "conscience." Even the part of speech is faulty. The record-breaking distribution and sales of the novel in July of 2015 was met with mixed reviews. Diane Johnson in "Daddy's Girl," a review of the novel in the *New York Review of Books* (September 24, 2015), wrote, "The first reactions were of wary disappointments," "cursory, often clumsy." Still, it enjoyed a brief few weeks on the *New York Times* bestseller list. Many ardent fans of *To Kill a Mockingbird* and Atticus vowed never to read it, especially attorneys who had been inspired by Atticus to enter the field of law.

Mick Brown, writing for the *Telegraph* (July 10, 2015) asked the question, "Would it have been kinder not to publish Harper Lee's *Go Set a Watchman*?" based on his reading of one chapter. "But one fears that those in search of the vivid and much-loved Scout are in for a disappointment. . . . perhaps it would have been a greater kindness to her reputation, and to the millions who cherish *To Kill a Mockingbird,* not to have published it at all."

Lauren Strickland contended that because, from all accounts, Nelle Harper was "in no state to approve the publication of *Go Set a Watchman*" and because she had never wanted anything else of hers published in her lifetime, it was unethical to read the novel ("Is It Ethical?").

Doris Forest, in a letter to the *New Yorker* of July 7, 2015, expressed the views of many Harper Lee fans: "I hope that readers of the novel will see it as a publisher's hustle at the expense of a beloved author, who unfortunately was in no position to stop its release."

Diane Johnson summed up all the extraliterary questions that attach themselves to the release of the second, "less accomplished" novel: the way in which it was discovered; the part of the editors of both novels; Nelle Harper's mental and physical condition; the quality of *Go Set a Watchman*; and where the millions of dollars it was bringing in were going.

On February 19, 2016, seven months after the publication of the novel, Nelle Harper died.

The announcement has been made that in the 2017–18 season, *To Kill a Mockingbird* will open on Broadway as a play produced by Scott Rudin. Plans are in the offing to turn Monroeville into a Harper Lee tourist center.

Further Reading

Alter, Alexandra. "A Collaboration in Mischief and More." *New York Times*, August 10, 2015, C1, C4.

Alter, Alexandra. "After 55 Years, a Sequel of Sorts by Harper Lee." *New York Times*, February 4, 2015, A1, A3.

Alter, Alexandra, and Serge Kovaleski. "After Harper Lee Novel Surfaces, Plots Arise." *New York Times*, February 8, 2015, A1, A3.

Blackwell, Louise. "Harper Lee." In *Southern Writers: A Biographical Dictionary*, edited by Joseph Flora and Louis Rubin. Baton Rouge: Louisiana State University Press, 1979.

Butts, Thomas Lane. Interview.

Capote, Truman. *In Cold Blood*. New York: Random House, 1993.

Capote, Truman. *Other Voices, Other Rooms*. New York: Vintage Press, 1948.

Cep, Casey. "Harper Lee's Abandoned True-Crime Novel." *New Yorker*, March 17, 2015. http://www.newyorker.com/books/page-turner/harper-lees-forgotten-true-crime-project.

Chandler, Kim. "Murder Mystery: What Happened to Harper Lee's True-Crime Novel?" *Huffington Post*, September 9, 2015. www.huffington post.com/entry/alabama-murder-mystery-what-happened-to-harper-lees-true-crime-novel.9/9/15.

Charles, Ron. "The Shame of Harper Lee's Muddled Legacy." *Washington Post*, Feb. 28, 2016, E5. www.washingtonpost.com/people/ron-charles.

Chen, Ginny. "14 Things You Didn't Know About Harper Lee's and Truman Capote's Friendship." n.d. https://www.barnesandnoble.com/blog/14-things-you-didnt-know-about-harper-lee-and-truman-capotes-friendship.

Clarke, Gerald. *Capote*. New York: Simon and Schuster, 1988.

Dunphy, Jack. *Dear Genius*. New York: McGraw-Hill, 1987.

Grimes, William. "'Mockingbird' Author, Elusive Voice of the Small Town South." *New York Times*, February 20, 2016, A1, C1.

Hensler, Philip. "Why Harper Lee Kept Her Silence for 55 Years." *The Telegraph*, February 19, 2016. http://www.telegraph.co.uk/books/go-set-a-watchman/why-harper-lee-kept-her-silence-for-55-years/.

Hill, Angela. "Harper Lee Hoopla Hits Stores." *Bay Area News Group*, July 13, 2015, 1, 6.

Johnson, Claudia Durst. *To Kill a Mockingbird: Threatening Boundaries*. New York: Twayne Publishers, 1994.

Jones, George Thomas. "Did Unwanted Fame Put Out Harper Lee's Flame?" *Monroe Journal*, March 1, 2016, 1, 2.

Kean, Danuta. "Harper Lee Estate Endorses *To Kill a Mockingbird* Graphic Novel." *The Guardian*, June 16, 2017. https://www.theguardian.com/books/2017/jun/06/harper-lee-estate-endorses-to-kill-a-mockingbird-graphic-novel.

Kellogg, Carolyn. "Alabama Closes Its Harper Lee Investigation." *Los Angeles Times*, April 3, 2015. http://www.latimes.com/books/jacketcopy/la-et-jc-harper-lee-alabama-officially-closes-investigation-20150403-story.html.

Kiselyak, Charles, dir. *Fearful Symmetry*. Universal Home Video, 1998. DVD.

Kovaleski, Serge, and Alexandra Alter. "Another Drama in Hometown of Harper Lee." *New York Times*, August 24, 2015, C1, C2.

Kovaleski, Serge, and Alexandra Alter. "Intrigue Grows Over New Book by Harper Lee." *New York Times*, July 3, 2015, A1, A3.

Kovaleski, Serge, Alexandra Alter, and Jennifer Crossley Howard. "State of Alabama Steps Into Debate of Harper Lee's Mental State." *New York Times*, March 12, 2015, A1, A16.

Lee, Harper. "Christmas to Me." *McCall's*, December 1961, 63.

Lee, Harper. *Go Set a Watchman*. New York: HarperCollins, 2015.

Lee, Harper. "Love—In Other Words." *Vogue*, April 15, 1961, 64–65.

Lee, Harper. *To Kill a Mockingbird*. Philadelphia: J. B. Lippincott, 1960. Warner Books paperback edition, 1982.

Life. The Enduring Power of To Kill a Mockingbird. Life Books, vol. 15, no. 9, June 26, 2015.

Mahler, Jonathan. "The Invisible Hand Behind Harper Lee's 'To Kill a Mockingbird'." *New York Times*, July 12, 2015. https://www.nytimes.com/2015/07/13/books/the-invisible-hand-behind-harper-lees-to-kill-a-mockingbird.html?_r=0.

McDonald, W. U. "Harper Lee's College Writings." *Notes and Queries*, May 1968, 131–32.

McGrath, Douglas, dir. *Infamous*. 2006; Warner Brothers, 2010. DVD.

Miller, Bennett, dir. *Capote*. 2005; Sony Pictures Entertainment, 2006. DVD.

Mills, Marja. "A Life Apart: Harper Lee, the Complex Woman Behind 'A Delicious Mystery.'" *Chicago Tribune*, September 13, 2002.

Mills, Marja. *The Mockingbird Next Door*. New York: Penguin, 2014.

Plimpton, George. Interview with Truman Capote. *New York Times Book Review*, January 16, 1966.

Severson, Kim. "Hometown Greets 'Watchman' Quietly." *New York Times*, July 15, 2015, C1, C5.

Shawn, Allen, and Wallace Shawn. "Mr. Shawn and Mr. Capote." *The New Yorker*, April 3, 2006, 5.

Shields, Charles. *Mockingbird: A Portrait of Harper Lee*. New York: Henry Holt, 2006.

Strickland, Lauren. "Is It Ethical to Read Harper Lee's 'Go Set a Watchman'?" *Lip Magazine*, July 20, 2015, 3. http://lipmag.com/featured/is-it-ethical-to-read-harper-lees-go-set-a-watchman/.

Suddath, Claire. "What Does Harper Lee Want?" *Bloomberg Business*, July 9, 2015. http://www.bloomberg.com/graphics/2015-harper-lee-go-set-a-watchman.

Voss, Ralph F. *Truman Capote and the Legacy of "In Cold Blood."* Tuscaloosa: University of Alabama Press, 2011.

CHAPTER TWO

Historical Context of
To Kill a Mockingbird and
Go Set a Watchman

At the heart of both *To Kill a Mockingbird* and *Go Set a Watchman* are economic and racial issues in the South, both strongly implied and specifically referenced. No reading of either book can even begin without some knowledge of the following, all of which are referred to frequently in the novels:

1. The Great Depression of the 1930s
2. The New Deal
3. The Scottsboro Boys trials, beginning in 1931 and continuing for decades
4. The extent of lynching in the first half of the 20th century
5. The everyday interactions of black and white people in a segregated South
6. The activities of the Ku Klux Klan
7. The rise of the White Citizens' Council
8. The character of the National Association for the Advancement of Colored People
9. *Brown v. Board of Education*
10. Rosa Parks and the Montgomery Bus Boycott
11. Autherine Lucy and the integration of the University of Alabama

The Great Depression

The social and economic climate that heightened racism in the 1930s is the setting of *To Kill a Mockingbird*. One sees the impact especially on the lives of the Cunninghams and other residents of Old Sarum and on the villainous Bob Ewell and his children. The Depression, which began in the popular imagination with a stock market crash in 1929 during the presidency of Herbert Hoover, but had existed long before that in rural areas, had a profound effect on every citizen of the United States. The value of stocks and businesses declined and remained at very low levels, causing grief to the businessman, to the workers he fired, to those he hired at starvation wages, and to farmers and sharecroppers. In Alabama and other rural areas, the Depression began earlier (1921) and lasted later than other parts of the country—for some into the 1940s. Historian Howard Zinn recounts: "By 1935, of 6,800,000 farmers, 2,800,800 were tenants. The average income of a sharecropper was $312 a year. Farm laborers, moving from farm to farm, area to area, no land of their own, in 1933 were earning about $300 a year" (388).

With people out of work or poorly paid, they were unable to buy goods and services, causing businesses to suffer even more. Scout describes Maycomb as a place where there was "nothing to buy and no money to buy it with" (5). Roughly 15,000 banks failed between 1921 and 1933, and customers, standing terrified in long lines outside to draw out their money, lost their life savings. The situation became a vicious cycle. It caused massive unemployment and families, unable to pay their mortgages, lost their farms and homes. In the 1930s, a total of 90,000 American businesses no longer had the money to operate. Three years after the 1929 crash, production in factories had dropped to 50 percent of what it had reached in the 1920s. This, of course, meant that factory workers lost their livelihoods. About one-fourth of the labor force lost its jobs. Thirty-seven percent of the nonagricultural workforce was left unemployed. The prices of agricultural products plummeted. Unemployment in the United States in the 1930s reached 15 million. Many of those who were listed as still employed were working only part-time. It has been estimated that an average of 5,000 people showed up for every 100 job openings.

Those lucky few who managed to find jobs also found that wages had dropped to sub-subsistence levels, even lower than they had been during the 1920s. It was a time when even a full-time employee, such as a mill worker, earned barely enough to live on. Wages were at rock bottom and conditions were brutal. One family of six working long hours in a Connecticut factory, for example, made a total of five dollars a week. In 1931 a person working 55 or 60 hours a week in Alabama would earn about $156 annually. Seamstresses working 16 hours a day received $10 a week. Some Massachusetts factories advertised that they would pay workers $4 or $5 a week. Men were making 5 cents an hour in sawmills; women 75 cents a week in sweatshops. One of the missionary ladies in *To Kill a Mockingbird* paid her maid $1.25 a week (233).

During Hoover's administration, there were no safety nets like unemployment insurance or food stamps to keep food on the table. There were no protections of bank savings, no social security benefits, no welfare, no subsidized health care. Starvation and malnutrition were commonplace throughout the country. People (some of them dressed like executives in suits) stood in long so-called bread lines or soup lines set up by private charities to get an allotment of food. Mention is made in *To Kill a Mockingbird* that the bread lines were growing longer in Birmingham, Alabama (116). The Welfare Council of New York City reported that 139 people, most of them children, died of starvation or malnutrition in that city alone in 1933. It was commonplace to see men on the streets and children in schools passing out from hunger. Hospitals complained that they were having to treat so many cases of severe malnutrition that they had little time or space to care for other ailments. Many families lived on one loaf of stale bread a day (at a cost of five cents), occasionally supplemented by dried beans.

Many people, primarily men and boys, rode the rails in an attempt to find work and escape the tragedies they found at home. Records show that in a single year, 693,000 people were thrown off boxcars. Photographs show well-dressed couples, among the displaced, hitchhiking to what they probably hoped would be a better life in another area. Whole extended families, thrown off their land like the Joads in John Steinbeck's novel *The Grapes of Wrath*, straggled across the country trying unsuccessfully to find work.

Throughout working-class neighborhoods in particular, the grim results of repossession and eviction were repeated. Families who couldn't make their rent or mortgage payments would come home to find all their possessions thrown in the street. People thrown out of their houses or off their land had to live in their cars, if they owned them. Many lived in what were called Hoovervilles, named for then President Herbert Hoover, who preceded Franklin Roosevelt. These were large communities, usually around urban centers, made up of makeshift sheds constructed from scraps—discarded slats, boxes, trash, and rags. The newspapers that the destitute used to cover themselves when they were sleeping were called Hoover blankets. (In *To Kill a Mockingbird,* mention is made of Hoover

Carts, usually cars, for which one could no longer buy gasoline, pulled by mules or horses.)

In many of the rural communities, especially in the Southwest, falling farm prices and the over-cultivation of soil, which literally blew away, had caused economic disaster long before the stock market crash of 1929. Sealing one's house tightly did not prevent dust from covering every conceivable surface overnight and naturally causing lung problems, particularly in young children. In Alabama, many farmers and farm workers moved to the cities of Birmingham, Huntsville, Anniston, and Montgomery hoping to find work. When this failed miserably, they moved back to their rural homes, along with thousands of former city dwellers, hoping to subsist off the land.

The Depression of the 1930s was just an episode in the life of abject poverty in the cotton-producing South. When crop prices and land prices plummeted and farmers could no longer pay their mortgages, banks foreclosed on them, repossessing their farms, evicting the people who lived there, and putting the farms up for auction. In the Midwest, sympathetic farmers turned to violence, attacking the bank managers and the sheriffs who carried out orders to displace farmers and sell their property. The farmers in the whole area showed up to stop auctions and hang nooses from the barn doors to discourage any person from bidding on a repossessed farm. In one instance in 1933 in Iowa, farmers forced the mortgage holder to accept a small token to settle the farmer's debt, then forced the broker to his knees to kiss the American flag.

In *To Kill a Mockingbird* we see the immediacy of this economic hardship in the poor children who attend Scout's school. Walter Cunningham and others come to school shoeless. Some of Scout's classmates are diseased, chiefly Burris Ewell: "He was the filthiest human I had ever seen. His neck was dark gray, the backs of his hands were rusty, and his fingernails were black deep into the quick" (27). The sight of lice on Burris and others cause the young teacher from northern Alabama to almost faint. Some are unable to attend school after an initial required first-day appearance because they have to work. Walter Cunningham explains to Atticus: "Reason I can't pass first grade, Mr. Finch, is I've had to stay out ever' spring an help Papa with the choppin'" (24). Some can't afford school lunches. Scout tries to explain the situation of Walter to her teacher—too poor to afford lunch money and too proud to accept help—and eventually takes him home to lunch with her family. Many of the fathers fed their families by hunting, both in and out of season. Like many poor but honest farmers, the Cunninghams—the family of Scout's schoolmate—pay for health and legal services with the produce they grow on their farms.

Dr. Reynolds "charges some folks a bushel of potatoes for delivery of a baby" (21).

Benjamin Meek Miller, elected to the governorship of Alabama in 1930, was known as "Old Economy" and was committed to balancing the budget and saving money. He inherited a broken state, requiring him to go against his theories to spend money on social services—but it was not enough to forestall greater disasters. President Roosevelt had to constantly push Miller to spend more of the money that the federal government provided to the state of Alabama for aid.

In *To Kill a Mockingbird*, Maycomb seems isolated from the labor disputes going on throughout the country, including those in Alabama. Scout mentions that even the state matters that Atticus had to deal with in the legislature "were remote from the world of Jem and me" (16). But in providing background on the Depression, "the sit-down strikes in Birmingham" (116) are mentioned. This is likely to be in reference to the national coal miner and steel worker strikes of 1933 and 1934, organized primarily by local unions with some outside radical help. The strikes became violent in Birmingham when owners turned machine guns on the miners (mostly black workers), and when the then governor, Bibb Graves, called out the National Guard. It was later found, in a Washington, DC, investigation that eleven of the National Guard officers involved were being paid by the Tennessee Coal, Iron, and Railroad Company in Alabama, the company against which the workers were striking (Hudson, *Black Worker in the Deep South*, 64, 65). During the early 1930s workers found to be union members were blacklisted. The only concession the miners received after their strikes was to be allowed to be active in their union. Historian Brian Kelly writes that Birmingham had become "a national symbol of urban suffering." Then, in 1935, the year of Tom Robinson's trial, the national CIO (Congress of Industrial Organizations) unionized the mine workers in Birmingham.

A significant number of radicals working to organize unions in Alabama during the 1930s were Communists who, among other endeavors, helped set up the Alabama Sharecroppers' Union made up primarily of black agricultural workers who were exploited by landowners. Though few in number, members of the organization became influential voices through strikes in the Black Belt of Alabama where Maycomb was located, helping to raise wages and improve conditions and agreements. Communists who were working for laborers both in the factories and on the farms were despised and attacked by the Ku Klux Klan, which held antilabor views.

In the South, this economic situation worsened the already ugly relations between poor whites and blacks who were competing for jobs. Poor whites often transferred their frustrations over the economic situation to poor blacks, blaming them for their problems and using them as scapegoats. Most labor unions were segregated. The Depression intensified upper- and middle-class fear that the underprivileged would rise up against them. To dampen strong and united union activity to improve appallingly low wages and working conditions, owners fanned the flames of racial discord, and rules and ordinances were passed to keep blacks and whites separated. This was especially true in Alabama's steel industry. The lower-class white animosity toward blacks, worsened by the economic situation, is unmistakable in Maycomb, Alabama.

President Roosevelt and the Beginning of the New Deal

In 1933 the presidency passed from Herbert Hoover, who had been vilified for his failure to alleviate suffering after the economy crashed in 1929, to Franklin Delano Roosevelt. A famous phrase from his first inaugural address is quoted on page six of *To Kill a Mockingbird*: "All we have to fear is fear itself."

Roosevelt immediately initiated policies called the New Deal, designed to put controls on businesses and banks and provide employment, relief, and dignity to ordinary citizens.

To provide help for relief efforts in the states, the Emergency Relief Act was passed in March of 1933, several months after FDR took office. Also in 1933, the Civilian Conservation Corps was enacted to put young men to work in parks and forests, eventually employing three million. Other laws were signed to investigate fraud in business, banks, and on Wall Street.

On June 16, 1933, Roosevelt signed one of the potentially most significant acts of the New Deal. It was called the NRA or National Recovery Act, designed to regulate business activities, including bans on child labor and rules on wages and work hours. This and subsequent laws to regulate child labor never covered agricultural labor, so it did improve the life of Scout's schoolmates. But on May 27 of 1935, the National Recovery Act was ruled unconstitutional by the United States Supreme Court. Scout declares that life in the Depression continues to be the same in Maycomb except for two big changes in 1935. "Firstly, people had removed from their store windows and automobiles the stickers that said NRA—WE DO OUR PART" (251). Atticus explains to her that the NRA is dead, and when she asked who killed it: "he said nine old men," meaning, of course, the Supreme Court (251).

Many of Roosevelt's New Deal programs still exist today, however, among them the Social Security Act; the Federal Deposit Insurance Corporation to insure bank deposits and reduce the number of bank failures; the regulatory Securities Exchange Act of 1934; the Wagner Act helping workers to unionize and negotiate with employers; the Tennessee Valley Authority, established to provide affordable power and flood control; and the Soil Conservation Act.

Eleanor Roosevelt, the president's wife, also mentioned in *To Kill a Mockingbird*, became an especially hated figure in the South because of her courageous activism in support of the rights of the poor, laborers, and black people. She, herself, joined a union when she wrote a newspaper column, and she traveled (often by herself in her car) to 48 states, supporting her husband's policies (which she had helped fashion), learning how the Depression was affecting ordinary black and white working people, and often visiting in the houses of the poor. Her presence would certainly have been felt in Scout's Alabama in her support of the Southern Tenant Farmers Union.

During the missionary meeting, Mrs. Merriweather, in castigating the behavior of black people, opines that their "uppity" behavior can be laid at the door of Eleanor Roosevelt: "I think that woman, that Mrs. Roosevelt's lost her mind—just plain lost her mind coming down to Birmingham and tryin' to sit with 'em. If I was the Mayor of Birmingham, I'd . . ." (234). In 1938, several years after the setting of *To Kill a Mockingbird*, Mrs. Roosevelt shocked the South by defying the laws of Birmingham, sitting in the aisle with black people at the Southern Conference for Human Welfare. As a coda, she also joined the National Association for the Advancement of Colored People (so despised in *Go Set a Watchman*) and supported the Montgomery Bus Boycott.

The Scottsboro Trials

It was in such a distressing social and economic climate that the racism of the Scottsboro case (and Tom Robinson's trial) unfolded. Tom Robinson's trial has striking parallels to the one of the most infamous court cases in American history. Both the fictional and the historical cases take place in the 1930s, a time of turmoil and change in America, and both are set in Alabama. In both, the defendants were black men and the accusers were white women. In both instances the charge was rape, which constituted, in the South, the most heinous crime imaginable and was often given as justification for brutal lynchings. Other substantial similarities between the fiction and the historical trials are apparent.

On March 25, 1931, several groups of white and black men and two white women were riding the rails from Tennessee to Alabama in various open and closed railroad cars designed to carry freight and gravel. At one point on the trip, some of the black and white men began fighting. There were conflicting reports later about who started the fight. A few black men threw all but one white man off the car. When the train arrived at the little junction of Paint Rock, Alabama, all those riding the rails, including nine black men, at least one white man, and the two white women, were arrested, probably on charges of vagrancy. It should be noted that the two women had to be chased down because they ran away from the police along with some of the black men. When the white women were captured, they immediately accused the black men of raping them in a railroad car carrying gravel (called chert).

Even within the hour, historian Dan T. Carter writes, word of the rape charges had spread, eventually reaching all of Alabama and adjoining states. In the afternoon, a lynching loomed immediately as hundreds of farmers gathered threateningly in front of the Scottsboro jail. These men match the description of the Old Sarum lynch mob in *To Kill a Mockingbird*: chewing tobacco and dressed in faded overalls. The sheriff argued with the mob and brought in further deputies. The mayor of Scottsboro also pleaded with them to disperse and let the law take its course. Attempts to secretly relocate the men failed when they discovered the mob had disabled the police vehicles. As threats from the crowd got louder and more frequent, the sheriff telephoned the governor in Montgomery who had run on an anti-lynching platform. He called the nearest state National Guard located in Guntersville to send 25 armed men to the scene. When they arrived at midnight, the crowd had diminished to just a few men sitting in their cars, and the threat was over.

The white women remained under arrest in jail for several days, pending charges of vagrancy and possible violation of the Mann Act (taking a minor across state lines for prostitution). Because the older woman, Victoria Price, was a known prostitute, the police were tipped off (very likely by the under-age Ruby Bates) that the two women were involved in some criminal act before they left Tennessee for Alabama. They were examined by physicians immediately upon their arrival in Scottsboro and released from jail after a few days. This medical evidence, which would have helped to exonerate the men, did not come forward until after several of the trials had been held.

As the trials progressed, both the NAACP and the Communist Party (the ILD or International Labor Defense) took interest in the defense, competing and quarreling with one another.

The trial of the nine men on charges of rape began on April 6, 1931, only 12 days after the arrests (a date, incidentally, that Harper Lee instantly recalled when I brought up the trial to her). On April 9, eight of the nine were found guilty and sentenced to death.

On November 7, 1932, the U.S. Supreme Court ordered new trials for the Scottsboro defendants because they lacked adequate legal representation. Meanwhile, the Scottsboro case became a *cause célèbre* among liberals and radicals in the North. Red diaper baby and former Communist Oscar Berland recalls marching with his fellow students in New York City, everyone carrying signs that read "Free the Scottsboro Boys." On March 27, 1933, the new trials ordered by the Court began in Decatur, Alabama, with the involvement of two distinguished participants: a famous New York City defense lawyer named Samuel S. Leibowitz, a major figure in the trials for over a decade, and Judge James E. Horton, who would fly in the face of community sentiment by the unusual actions he took in the summer of 1933.

In this second attempt to resolve the case, the retrial for the first defendant lasted almost two weeks instead of the few hours it had in 1931. And this time the chief testimony included the detailed reports of two physicians, whose examinations of the women within two hours of the alleged crimes refuted the likelihood that multiple rapes had occurred on a bed of gravel. A young doctor, Marvin Lynch, told Judge Horton in private: "I looked at both the women and told them they were lying, that they knew they had not been raped . . . and they just laughed at me" (interview with James Edwin Horton, in Carter, *Scottsboro*, 215). But Dr. Lynch, unlike the other physician, Dr. Bridges, refused to testify on the stand for fear that it would ruin his new practice.

Testimony was also given by the younger woman, Ruby Bates, who now denied in court that she or her friend, Victoria Price, had ever been raped. As a result of this, as well as of material brought out by investigations and by cross-examinations of the witnesses, the character and honesty of accuser Victoria Price came under more careful scrutiny. Afterward, Ruby Bates regularly joined Communist rallies in New York City and Washington, DC, protesting the imprisonment of the defendants.

On April 9, 1933, the first of the defendants, Haywood Patterson, was again found guilty of rape and sentenced to execution. But the execution was delayed and six days after the original date set for Patterson's execution, one of the most startling events in this Southern trial took place: the judge, James Horton, effectively overturned the conviction of the jury and, in a meticulous analysis of the evidence that had been presented, ordered a new trial on the grounds that the evidence presented did not warrant conviction. It is probably not a coincidence that Judge Horton lost an election in the fall following his verdict.

Despite Judge Horton's unprecedented action in a Southern court, the second defendant, Clarence Norris, was tried in late 1933 and found guilty as charged, but his execution was delayed pending appeal, and he was later placed on parole. The intolerable living and working conditions of his parole prompted him to escape to the North where he remained hidden.

During this time all the rest of the defendants remained in prison, and not for two more years was any further significant action taken as Leibowitz filed repeated appeals to higher courts. Finally, on April 1, 1935, the United States Supreme Court reversed the convictions of defendants Patterson and Norris on the grounds that qualified black people had been systematically excluded from all juries in Alabama, and had been specifically excluded in this case. They were excluded, of course, because they were not on voting rolls, having been denied the right to vote. (Note the extended discussion of the make-up of juries in *To Kill a Mockingbird*.) As a result of the Supreme Court decision, one black man was placed on the jury.

Still, even this decision by the Supreme Court was not the end of the trials, for on May 1, 1935, Victoria Price swore out new warrants against the men. By 1940 charges against four men were dropped and all but one of them either escaped or were paroled. In June of 1950, this last defendant in jail, Andrew Wright, was released from prison and in October of 1976, the then remaining defendant, Clarence Norris, was pardoned by the state of Alabama, now, ironically under the governorship of George Wallace, after years of hiding in New York City, keeping his whereabouts secret even from his family members in the North, lest he be found out. Norris was told that he would be given a pardon if he returned to Alabama to receive it, but wisely replied that he would not return to Alabama until he had the pardon in his hands. The pardon was provided to him before he came to Alabama ceremoniously to meet with officials.

The obvious parallels to Harper Lee's novel, in addition to time, place, and charges, are the threats of lynching in both cases, the similarity between Judge Horton and Atticus, the issue of juries, and that the accusers in both the Scottsboro and Tom Robinson's case were poor women who had secrets that the charges of rape were intended to cover up, making their veracity an issue.

Lynching

A lynching is defined as an illegal execution of a person by a group, without benefit of law or trial. Some victims had not been arrested and some were pulled from jails, often tortured and mutilated before being either burned alive, shot by firing squads, or hanged. Attempts have been made to record these murders by the NAACP beginning in 1912, and later by Tuskegee University, which recorded 4,733 deaths by lynching between 1882 and 1959, and then by the Montgomery-based Equal Justice Initiative. In 73 years, from 1877 to 1950, there were 300 documented lynchings of black people in Alabama alone: between 1882 and 1962, there were 29 lynchings in Jefferson County. Monroe County, the setting of both of Harper Lee's novels, had the second most—18.

Not only were these killings (overwhelmingly of black males) outside the judicial/legal system, they were frequently done when no crime had been committed by their target, but instead for such charges as speaking inappropriately to a white person or bumping into a white person. About 1 percent of these white murderers were convicted. As in the historical Scottsboro trials and in *To Kill a Mockingbird*, lynching was threatened and rationalized as a necessary way to protect white women from black men.

The scenes of lynchings were often photographed, and sometimes made into postcards. These photographs are evidence that lynchings came to be social events regarded as public entertainment. Whole white families, including women and children, attended. In one infamous photograph, young girls are laughing in the front row of a mob watching the hanging body of a black man.

It was the lower-class Old Sarum residents who tried to engineer the lynching of Tom in *To Kill a Mockingbird*, and this scenario seems to have been customary. Community leaders and professionals, like Atticus, and the mayor of Scottsboro in the historical trials, often tried unsuccessfully to prevent lynching. One example of this occurred in Greenwood, South Carolina, in 1906 when a mob surrounded a black man who had cut, but not killed, a black woman with a weapon and threatened a white woman. The state's Governor Heyward made a long trip from the capital in Columbia to Greenwood, at the behest of business leaders, to plead for the mob to let the law take its course. The town's bank president and mill owner also faced off the mob, threatening to close the mills, in which most of the mob worked, if the lynching happened. These men were unsuccessful in stopping the killing, One of the horrendous racial events that occurred around the time of Jean Louise's visit home in *Go Set a Watchman*, and seems to be referenced in the novel as "that Mississippi business," was the lynching of Emmett Till, a black 14-year-old, in 1955.

Till, who was from Chicago, was visiting relatives in Mississippi. He had grown up in the largely segregated South Side of Chicago, and was not versed in the racial etiquette of the Deep South. At a country store, on a dare, he bought some candy, and on the way out, said, "Bye, Baby" to the white woman behind the counter.

She told her husband and others that Till had made sexual advances to her (charges which, 62 years later, she recanted). On the basis of her story, her husband and his brother-in-law went to the home of Till's relatives, forced him into their car, beat and mutilated him beyond recognition, killed him, and dumped him in the Tallahatchie River. His killers were tried and found not guilty by an all-white jury. Timothy B. Tyson writes in *The Blood of Emmett Till* that he had paid the released killers to tell their story, about which they showed no remorse.

The Daily Lives of Black People

Injustice in the courts and the constant threat of lynching were just the most egregious of the burdens of black people in the South. Racial segregation had always been a way of life. Blacks and whites went to separate schools, separate churches, separate clothing stores, and separate hospitals. They lived in separate neighborhoods and separate housing complexes. They were treated by separate doctors and separate dentists and had no access to public institutions of higher education where white people were in attendance. They had separate waiting rooms in all offices and bus and train stations, separate rest rooms, and even separate water fountains. White people had access to restaurants, motels, hotels, parks, and other recreational facilities that black people were not allowed to use. It was rare for a black person to find a place to sit down and eat or sleep away from home. Facilities like the YMCA and YWCA were for whites only. They were restricted to one "blacks-only" car on trains and the balconies of movie houses.

The ritual required of black bus riders in Montgomery, Alabama, was customary everywhere in the South. Most bus passengers were black people. They had to step into the bus and buy a ticket from the driver in the front, then step out of the bus and walk to the rear entrance, where they boarded and then sat in the back. If all the seats were taken in the back half of the bus and a seat was available in the white section near the front, the black passenger still had to stand. If a white passenger boarded the bus and no seat was available, the black passenger nearest the front of the bus was expected to rise, give her seat to the white passenger, and then stand. If she did not do this voluntarily, the bus driver ordered her to, calling out from his place at the front of the bus. Moreover, every black person in that row of seats on both sides of the aisle was expected to rise and stand so that the white passenger would not be sitting in the same row as black passengers.

Black women who worked as maids, cooks, or nurses in the houses of whites were expected to eat in the kitchen or on the back porch, separate from the white family for whom they had cooked the meal. If the white employer preferred to take her lunch in the kitchen, the housekeeper ate at a separate table in the same kitchen—or she ate standing up, or after the white person had finished and left the kitchen. Black men were usually not allowed to eat in the houses of whites at all: food was handed to them out the back door on paper plates or in pans and jars kept for that specific purpose.

Racial discrimination in hiring was open and above board, applications often being stamped "whites only." Jobs for black men were restricted to common labor or servicing the black community only. The only professional jobs open to educated black men and women were the ministry and teaching in black schools.

Well into the second half of the 20th century, ugly protests kept blacks out of white churches. When a Southern Baptist minister, with a church near Birmingham, asked the congregations to welcome *all* deaf people to the church where the service would be augmented by sign language, some were suspicious and outraged that he meant black deaf people as well, and he was insulted and isolated and eventually encouraged to leave.

Black people were specifically barred from supervisory positions and jobs as fire fighters, police officers, and bus drivers.

In less concrete but more humiliating matters of personal dignity and self-esteem, black people suffered as well. Adults, no matter how old, were always and only addressed by their first names by white adults and children alike. No matter what their age, they were expected to address any white person over the age of 12 as Mr. or Miss or Mrs. Note that Scout questions Calpurnia about her sudden practice of calling Jem "Mr. Jem" when he reaches adolescence. Grown black males were invariably called boys.

This was the world of the South in both *To Kill a Mockingbird* and *Go Set a Watchman*.

The Ku Klux Klan

Three organizations pertinent to the race struggle are brought up in *To Kill a Mockingbird* and *Go Set a Watchman*: the Ku Klux Klan, the White Citizens' Council, and the NAACP.

Atticus discounts the influence of the Klan in both novels. In *To Kill a Mockingbird*, he describes the Klan as a bunch of clowns that are not worth worrying about. In *Go Set a Watchman*, it is revealed to Jean Louise that at one time long before the present action, Atticus had actually joined the Klan for a time, the rationalization being that he wanted to find out what their mindset and concerns were.

The Klan, which was originally founded in 1866 as a social club in Pulaski, Tennessee, chiefly by Confederate veterans, assumed the name "The Invisible Empire" in 1867 and spread throughout the South in the 1870s. Historians identify three distinct Klans: the founding one; the second, operating from 1915 to 1944; and the third one from 1946 to the present. The Klan had distinct beliefs, the most important being:

White supremacist, anti-black, and anti-immigrant convictions;

Anti-Catholic and anti-Jewish biases;

Toleration of undercover violence, including torture and murder, to keep undesirables "in their places."

To hide their identities and terrorize the general populace, their costumes, inspired by the 1915 film *The Birth of a Nation*, were white sheets and white masks with conical white headgear.

These so-called knight riders early turned to lynching, beatings, bombings, cross-burnings, and other crimes against blacks and some whites who violated the Klan's moral code, especially the separation of the races. In 1927 the Klan mounted a reign of terror in Alabama. The organization was responsible for three lynchings of black people in 1940, including Alabamian Jesse Thornton, whose crime was failing to address a policeman as "mister." The organization was behind bombings in Alabama of houses and churches in the 1930s, 1940s, and 1950s. One section of Birmingham, College Hill, was bombed so often that it was referred to as "Dynamite Hill." In 1951 and 1952, the houses of 40 black families were bombed by the Klan in Alabama.

Still, in the South, they claimed to work for political reforms and better schools and conditions for lower-class citizens. And a few so-called "respectable" people were Klan members. Most religious denominations refused to support the Klan, but Brian R. Farmer writes that many of its members were ministers. Hugo Black, an Alabama attorney from an humble background, who was a senator and sworn onto the U.S. Supreme Court in 1937, had been a member of the Ku Klux Klan from 1923 to 1925, having joined because he thought it would further his political career.

The White Citizens' Council

In July of 1954, after the United State Supreme Court overturned the earlier "separate but equal" law in *Brown v. Board of Education* and ruled that public schools should be integrated, local groups of the racist White Citizens' Council sprang up in the South. This was about three years before Jean Louise's visit home to Maycomb in *Go Set a Watchman* where she then slips into a meeting of Maycomb's Citizens' Council.

They were considered a more civilized, "respectable" version of the Klan. Their numbers included professionals, businessmen, public officials, police officers and sheriffs, and some religious leaders. They were formed to oppose voting rights for black people and racial integration in public places. They usually did not stoop to the violence of the Klan, though in 1963, a black civil rights leader named Medgar Evers was murdered by a man who was a member of both the Klan and the White Citizens' Council in Mississippi, and the WCC paid his expenses for two trials. Unlike the Klan, the WCC operated openly and had the demeanor, as Charles M. Payne wrote, of a Rotary Club (34–35). The WCC was also called the "gentleman's version" of the Klan. In Montgomery, Alabama, in 1955, during the bus boycott, all three members of the Montgomery City Commission publicly announced that they had become members of the WCC, as did Police Commissioner Clyde Sellers and the mayor. Montgomery membership reached 10,000 by the end of February of that year.

In 1956, the WCC was able to force the passage of a broad segregation law in Louisiana, which was signed by the governor. U.S. senator for Mississippi, James Eastland, spoke to a WCC rally. After Autherine Lucy's ouster at the University of Alabama, Montgomery, Alabama, had the biggest rally in its history with some 15,000 celebrants.

Because their members held economic control over communities, their vengeful actions against those who tried to register to vote or spoke out against Jim Crow segregation included insisting that mortgages be paid in full, throwing tenants out of their homes, refusing to issue loans, blacklisting, firing, and boycotting businesses owned by or employing black people. In Yazoo City, Mississippi, in 1955, the names of 53 people who had signed a petition for school integration were made public by the local paper. As a result, those who signed lost their jobs and their ability to get credit.

Many Southern newspapers supported the WCC and, by the late 1950s, the organization published its own newspaper. The WCC began to circulate the story that the bombings of the houses of E. D. Nixon and Martin Luther King had been arranged by black leaders to create sympathy for themselves. In the 1950s, at the time of Jean Louise's exposure to the WCC, which Atticus and Henry had joined, the Council put out religious books for children showing a segregated heaven.

The National Association for the Advancement of Colored People

The National Association for the Advancement of Colored People, or the NAACP, is mentioned repeatedly in *Go Set a Watchman*. The nonviolent organization was founded in 1909 by W. E. B. Du Bois, among others, with the purpose of bringing racial discrimination to an end and securing rights and equality. Its initial branch in Alabama was set up in Talladega in 1915. During the first half of the 20th century, its chief targets were lynching and disenfranchisement. Its legal defense fund was founded in 1940, and it was known throughout the 20th century for its strong and aggressive litigation and its publicized use of education, lobbying, and working for legislation to further its causes. Clearly, in the South, where Jim Crow segregation and disenfranchisement of blacks were enshrined in law, the NAACP was unwelcome.

In the 1930s, the setting of *To Kill a Mockingbird*, the NAACP's presence was felt in Alabama when it became involved in raising funds for the defense of the Scottsboro Boys. In the 1940s, the organization was briefly successful in winning a case giving blacks access to primaries. After World War II, membership and activity surged when black veterans returned from Europe to their segregated homes in the South where they still were not allowed to exercise their right to vote. Hundreds left the South, but some of those who remained worked with the NAACP.

One of the NAACP's major efforts was to make segregation illegal in public schools and other public places in the South. As *Go Tell a Watchman* suggests, its legal expertise became apparent after the 1954 Supreme Court decision, *Brown v. Board of Education*, which it had filed in 1951 and to which it had devoted its skill and funding.

In 1958, after the bus boycott in Montgomery, Alabama, Alabama banned NAACP activity within the state. The ruling was challenged in the U.S. Supreme Court in *NAACP v. Alabama*, and the court ruled in favor of the organization and against the state.

As the NAACP had had disagreements in the 1930s with the more aggressive Communist Party and labor unions, so it conflicted in the 1950s and 1960s with other civil rights organizations that had begun springing up—organizations that used civil disobedience and public protests, strategies of which the NAACP disapproved. Still, it continued to be regarded as a despised enemy in the South because of its legal successes in the area of civil rights.

One of the most prominent NAACP figures in Alabama was a Birmingham resident named Arthur Shores, whose life reflects much of the history of the organization in Alabama. Shores was an active NAACP attorney—the only black practicing attorney in Alabama at one time—who challenged Birmingham's segregated zoning laws, was appointed to the Jefferson County Democratic Executive Committee (after a successful lawsuit in 1952), and who filed a suit on behalf of Autherine Lucy to integrate the University of Alabama. In August of 1963, his house was bombed.

Brown v. Board of Education

The Supreme Court decision toward which the nation's racist turmoil had been building for decades was *Brown v. Board of Education*, mentioned often and discussed in *Go Set a Watchman*. The decision rocked Harper Lee's native state of Alabama just when she was thinking about and beginning to write the story of unequal justice in a small town there. In *Go Set a Watchman*, it is the primary issue on which her relationship with her father pivots.

Some background reveals its complexity. The 14th Amendment to the Constitution of the United States, passed in 1868, gave all citizens of the nation equal rights and denied any state the power to "abridge the privileges or immunities of citizens of the United States." But in 1896, a Supreme Court decision was handed down in *Plessy v. Ferguson* that lent "separate but equal" segregation the sanction of law. As long as public facilities for blacks and whites were equal, the Court decided, they could be separate.

But inequalities, especially in public education, had long been a fact of life, as one sees illustrated in *To Kill a Mockingbird* when few black people could read and only because they were self-taught or privately taught—like Calpurnia and her son Zeebo. Calpurnia learned to read from a woman in the family for whom she worked and from law books in the Finches' house and she herself teaches her son to read and write. Especially after World War II, struggles were waged in many counties throughout the nation where, even if separate schools existed, black children often lacked buses, desks, and books and were housed in leaking, unheated buildings.

In 1949, in Clarendon County, South Carolina, black citizens began what would become a series of suits for equality of education for their children. The instigating circumstance was the decision by the county's all-white board of education to take away the one school bus for black children in order to add it to a fleet of 30 school buses for white children. The cases that were brought to court as a result of agitation in Clarendon County were stepping stones to *Brown v. Board of Education*.

In June of 1950, civil rights activists won victories for black people seeking equal treatment in several cases before the Supreme Court, but segregation itself was not seriously challenged. Still, the question kept arising over whether separate facilities would or could ever be equal. Limited desegregation had occurred in postgraduate education around the country: in Texas, at the University of Maryland, and in Louisiana State University, the University of Virginia, and the University of North Carolina. In some parts of the South, including Alabama, black college graduates were not admitted to any professional or graduate schools like law, medicine, and education. Jim McWilliams, who had been raised in a steel mill family outside of Birmingham, was helped by his teachers to attend the all-black college of Tuskegee in Alabama. When he expressed interest in the study of law after he graduated, there was no law school in the state that would accept a black student. But to stave off integration, in Alabama, as in other Southern states, the state would pay to send such students to other states where prospective law students, for example, could receive law degrees. And so, McWilliams received his legal education at the University of Michigan, at Alabama's expense in the 1950s.

By the time the case for equal education in Clarendon County reached the federal court in Charleston, South Carolina, Thurgood Marshall, the prosecuting attorney, and his staff, decided to attack segregation itself—as well as unequal school facilities—to argue that segregation was an evil that necessarily created inequalities. Separate, they would argue, could not be equal.

Although the court decided in favor of sustaining school segregation in South Carolina in June of 1951, another trial challenging school segregation was already under way in Topeka, Kansas, charging that segregation amounted to inequality. A black man—Oliver Brown—lent his name to the suit charging that segregation in the Topeka schools constituted unequal treatment. The suit failed in district court, but it was the expressed legal opinion of the higher court that segregation labeled black children as inferior and adversely affected their motivation to learn. One judge explained years later that the court believed a district court could not legally strike down *Plessy v. Ferguson*, a Supreme Court decision that upheld separate but equal. The highest court in the land, the one that had rendered the decision in *Plessy*, would have to be the Court to strike it down.

Finally, on May 17, 1954, after hearing several cases that together came to be identified as *Brown v. Board of Education*, the United States Supreme Court announced that by unanimous decision, the "separate but equal" doctrine of *Plessy v. Ferguson* would no longer be the law of the land.

The decision and the ensuing struggle in the South to negate or ignore it deeply affected all Americans.

Segregationists and many strict Constitutionalists, like Atticus, objected that *Brown* violated the states' rights guaranteed in the 10th Amendment. In an awkward and inconsistent moment in the novel, even Jean Louise says the decision initially angered her because she thought there should have been a more constitutionally correct avenue to accomplish the same thing.

Montgomery Bus Boycott

One of the most important events in civil rights history began on December 1, 1955, in Montgomery, Alabama, where Atticus had served in the state legislature, at a time when Harper Lee was working on her two novels, just two years before the action of *Go Set a Watchman*. The crisis was put in motion when a black seamstress named Rosa Parks, weary from a day of working as a tailor's assistant in a department store, boarded a city bus to go home. Parks, who, incidentally, was already involved in civil rights activism, sat in an empty seat near the back of the white section of the bus. When a white man boarded the bus after all the seats for whites had been taken, the blacks in the row where Rosa Parks had taken her seat were ordered to give up their seats and stand so that the white man could have a seat. All except Mrs. Parks did as they were told. When she refused, she was arrested. Within hours, a boycott of all city buses was being planned. A black leader, E. D. Nixon, suggested that Rosa Parks take her case to court.

On December 6, black citizens refused to ride the system's buses until a "first-come, first served" policy was put into effect. This was the position of the black leadership of the city that included a young pastor, Martin Luther King Jr. Participation in the boycott was extremely high because most bus riders were black, and the bus system began to feel the intense economic pressure of losing 90 percent of its passengers. Rates were increased, and white people who were seen giving rides to black people were routinely ticketed. Violent opposition to the boycotters broke out, crosses were burned, jobs were lost, but still the boycott continued. On January 30, a bomb exploded on Martin Luther King's front porch.

On February 1, a class action suit was filed in U.S. District Court asking that state laws mandating segregation on public vehicles be judged unconstitutional, in effect calling for an end to segregation on city buses. On February 21 and 22, 1956, warrants were issued for the arrest of 115 leaders of the boycott, yet further peaceful rallies and demonstrations were held. On March 22 King was found guilty of violating the state anti-boycott laws. Not until over a year after the boycott began was a resolution reached when buses were desegregated.

Though a battle was won, the story did not end on a happy note. White bus riders were furious, some lashing out verbally with racist slurs. At one point a white rider slapped a black woman. Dummies labeled NAACP were hanged in effigy in downtown Montgomery. A 15-year-old black girl waiting at a bus stop was surrounded and beaten by five white men. Black men and women were the targets of gunshots. A pregnant woman was shot in both legs. Shots were fired into Martin Luther King's house. The violence spread from Montgomery to Birmingham. In Montgomery, on January 10, 1957, bombs were set off in four black churches and two houses.

Author David Aretha repeats the story of a white woman, Montgomery librarian Juliette Morgan, who had written letters to the newspaper supporting integration and the bus boycott. When one of her letters of praise of a white integrationist was published in the paper, she was harassed with hate letters and phone calls, cross burnings in her yard, and she was shunned by friends and neighbors. Even her library was boycotted by whites. Unable to endure this treatment, she took her own life on July 15, 1957.

Autherine Lucy and the University of Alabama

During the winter of 1956, at the same time that the Montgomery bus boycott was taking place, another ground-breaking series of events in the civil rights struggle was unfolding at the University of Alabama in Tuscaloosa. Harper Lee attended the university, during which time she had written for a student newspaper parodying racism. The time of the event coincided with Harper Lee's work on her two novels and is mentioned in *Go Set a Watchman* in one of Jean Louise's conversations during Aunt Alexandra's coffee party. Ever since 1953, civil rights leaders had been trying to arrange for the admission of a black student to Alabama's major state university. Some stories indicate that Ms. Lucy was admitted by mistake; others that the university had determined to choose between two women, one of whom was Autherine Lucy. The second prospective student was denied admission at an early stage on the specious grounds that she was married. Finally, in the winter of 1956, Autherine Lucy was officially notified that she had been admitted to the university as a graduate student.

When she arrived on campus to begin her classwork, her first day seemed to proceed pleasantly and without incident as many students supported and welcomed her. But she was informed that she could neither stay in the university dormitory nor eat in the university cafeteria, instigating a lawsuit against the university for discrimination.

Before the issue could be resolved, violence erupted on the campus and in the streets of Tuscaloosa on Friday night after her first day of class, and she had to be moved out of town. The *Birmingham News* counted as many as 1,000 people in the streets of University Avenue in Tuscaloosa. General rioting, including cross-burnings, damage to property, and attacks on black citizens, continued for three days. Later, investigators, with photographs and interviews, found that comparatively few students had been among the perpetrators.

Subsequent investigations identified most of the mob as employees of a local tire factory and students from a nearby high school. A cross was burned in the middle of University Avenue and firecrackers and smoke bombs were exploded. The song they sang was "Dixie." The chant was "Keep 'Bama White. To Hell with Autherine." The flag waved was the Confederate flag. Student leaders, including fraternity men, walked through the mob, trying, to no avail, to reason with them to cease the demonstration. Mobs ravaged the campus day and night, on the third day pelting Autherine Lucy with eggs and shattering the window of the car in which she was riding, forcing her to take shelter in Birmingham. At this time, the university's Board of Trustees moved to ban her from campus, on the grounds that her attendance was putting both her and the university at risk. Throughout the spring there were court hearings and appeals for her readmission, and many students at the university argued for her return to campus.

Hester, one of the magpies at the coffee party arranged by Aunt Alexandra in *Go Set a Watchman*, has absorbed a number of strange ideas about the affair from her husband, Bill. She asserts that fraternity boys ran Autherine off campus after some awful professors had tried to work up support for her admission. She links the Autherine Lucy debacle with Communist subversion. Communists, she declares, will do anything and are actively engaged in Alabama in their ultimate aim to "get hold of this country." She contends that they are sneaky like the "Catholics" in infiltrating the lower classes and black culture. Hester is convinced that Communists are all around, even in Maycomb. It is her husband Bill's conviction that there is a Communist "cell" in Tuscaloosa, stirring up the Autherine Lucy case. When Jean Louise challenges her, Hester asks, "What do you read, the *Worker*?" (a radical left-wing organ) (175).

There were, in fact, a few Communists working for labor rights and civil rights in Birmingham in the 1950s. Most of them were restricted to

Birmingham and worked undercover in the steel and iron industries. One such former member of the Communist Party remembers that he distributed pamphlets identifying a bomber of a black family's house as a policeman. He was immediately caught and arrested (Berland interview). But Communists were few in number in the early 1950s and disappeared by mid-decade after Bull Connor, commissioner of public safety for the city of Birmingham, made Communism illegal. There is no evidence to be found that there was a Communist "cell" in Tuscaloosa.

In conclusion, the various social, legal, and economic events of the 1930s and 1950s, mentioned in Harper Lee's two novels, are evidence of their importance in any literary discussion because these events are at the heart of both works.

Further Reading

Abernathy, Ralph David. *And the Walls Came Tumbling Down*. New York: Harper & Row, 1989.

Aretha, David. *Montgomery Bus Boycott*. Greensboro, NC: Morgan Reynolds Publishing, 2009.

Carr, Charles E. Jr. *On the Road to Freedom: A Guided Tour of the Civil Rights Movement*. Chapel Hill, NC: Algonquin Books, 2008.

Carter, Dan T. *Scottsboro: A Tragedy of the American South*. 2nd ed. Baton Rouge: Louisiana State University Press, 1984.

Cash, W. J. *The Mind of the South*. New York: Alfred A. Knopf, 1941.

Cason, Clarence. *90° in the Shade*. 1935. Reprint. Tuscaloosa: University of Alabama Press, 1983.

Clark, Culpepper. *The Schoolhouse Door: Segregation's Last Stand at the University of Alabama*. Oxford: Oxford University Press, 1993.

Cook, Blanche Wiesen. *Eleanor Roosevelt*. Vol. 3: *The War Years and After, 1939–1962*. New York: Viking, 2016.

Currie, Stephen. *The Birmingham Church Bombings*. Farmington Hills, MI: Lucent Books, 2006.

Farmer, Brian R. *American Political Ideologies*. Jefferson, NC: McFarland, 2006.

Feldman, Glenn. *Politics, Society, and the Klan in Alabama, 1915–1949*. Tuscaloosa: University of Alabama Press, 1999.

Flynt, Wayne. *Alabama in the Twentieth Century*. Tuscaloosa: University of Alabama Press, 2004.

Flynt, Wayne. *Poor But Proud: Alabama's Poor Whites*. Tuscaloosa: University of Alabama Press, 1989.

Gaillard, Frye. *Cradle of Freedom: Alabama and the Movement That Changed America*. Tuscaloosa: University of Alabama Press, 2004.

Gore, Leada. "Lynching Claimed 326 African American Lives in Alabama." *AL. com*, February 11, 2015. http://www.al.com/opinion/index.ssf/2015/02 /lynchings_claimed_326_african.html.

Greenhaw, Wayne. *Fighting the Devil in Dixie: How Civil Rights Activists Took on the Ku Klux Klan in Alabama.* Chicago: Lawrence Hill Books, 2011.

Grey, Fred D. *Bus Ride to Justice.* Montgomery, AL: Black Belt Press, 1995.

Hudson, Hosea. *Black Worker in the Deep South.* New York: International Publishers, 1972.

Jeffries, Hasan Kwame. *Bloody Lowndes: Civil Rights and Black Power in Alabama's Black Belt.* New York: New York University Press, 2009.

Kellogg, Charles Flint. *NAACP: A History of the National Association for the Advancement of Colored People.* Baltimore: Johns Hopkins University Press, 1967.

Kelley, Robin D. G. *Hammer and Hoe: Alabama Communists during the Great Depression.* Chapel Hill: University of North Carolina Press, 1990.

Kelly, Brian. "Organized Labor in Alabama." *Encyclopedia of Alabama.* http:// www.encyclopediaofalabama.org/article/h-1835.

Kelly, Brian. *Race, Class, and Power in the Alabama Coalfields, 1908–21.* Urbana: University of Illinois Press, 2001.

Kluger, Richard. *Simple Justice: The History of Brown v. Board of Education and Black America's Struggle for Equality.* New York: Alfred A. Knopf, 1976.

Lash, Joseph P. *Eleanor and Franklin.* New York: W. W. Norton, 1971.

Lee, Helen Shores, and Barbara S. Shores. *The Gentle Giant of Dynamite Hill.* Grand Rapids, MI: Zondervan Press, 2012.

McMillen, Neil R. *The Citizens' Council: Organized Resistance to the Second Reconstruction, 1954–64.* Urbana: University of Illinois Press, 1994.

McWhorter, Diane. *Carry Me Home: Birmingham, Alabama—The Climactic Battle of the Civil Rights Revolution.* New York: Simon and Schuster, 2001.

Norris, Clarence. *The Last of the Scottsboro Boys: An Autobiography.* New York: G. P. Putnam, 1979.

Oates, Stephen B. *Let the Trumpet Sound: The Life of Martin Luther King, Jr.* New York: Harper & Row, 1982.

Payne, Charles M. *I've Got the Light of Freedom: The Organizing Tradition and the Mississippi Freedom Struggle.* Berkeley: University of California Press, 2017.

"Record of Lynching in Alabama from 1871–1920." Alabama Department of Archives and History, Tuskegee Normal and Industrial Institute, n.d. http://digital.archives.alabama.gov/cdm/landingpage/collection/voices. Accessed 7/19/2017.

Rice, Arnold S. *The Ku Klux Klan in American Politics.* New York: Haskell House, 1962.

Robinson, Jo Ann Gibson. *The Montgomery Bus Boycott and the Women Who Started It.* Knoxville: University of Tennessee Press, 1987.

Sherrill, Robert. *Gothic Politics in the Deep South: Stars of the New Confederacy.* New York: Ballantine, 1968.

Tyson. Timothy B. *The Blood of Emmett Till.* New York: Simon and Schuster, 2017.

Wade, Wyn Craig. *The Fiery Cross: The Ku Klux Klan in America.* New York: Oxford University Press, 1998.

Watkins, T. H. *The Great Depression: America in the 1930s.* Boston: Little Brown, 1993.

Wiggins, Sarah Woolfolk, ed. *From Civil War to Civil Rights: Alabama, 1860–1960.* Tuscaloosa: University of Alabama Press, 1987.

Williamson, Joel. *A Rage for Order: Black/White Relations in the American South since Emancipation.* Oxford: Oxford University Press, 1986.

Zangrando, Robert L. *The NAACP's Crusade against Lynching.* Philadelphia: Temple University Press, 1980.

Zinn, Howard. *A People's History of the United States, 1492–Present.* New York: HarperCollins, 1980.

CHAPTER THREE

Literary Structure and Themes of *To Kill a Mockingbird* and *Go Set a Watchman*

Some complications arise from analyzing Harper Lee's two novels, in that *Go Set a Watchman*, having been written before *To Kill a Mockingbird*, takes place 20 years after and was published some 55 years later. For discussion, the novels will be examined in chronological order of their plots and publication—*To Kill a Mockingbird* followed by *Go Set a Watchman*.

The Entwined Points of View

Harper Lee's *Go Set a Watchman*, published in 2015, shares the setting of Maycomb, Alabama, and many of the same characters and issues with *To Kill a Mockingbird* (1960), but the structures of the two novels are decidedly different.

Both novels are from the point of view of the same character. The first is Scout; the second is Jean Louise, "Scout" having been her childhood nickname. The point of view in *To Kill a Mockingbird* is the most complex, since, while the book is written by an adult, it is limited but enhanced by being seen through the eyes of the elementary school–aged Scout. In that more is revealed through the child's eyes than she herself understands, it is an ironic narration.

Go Set a Watchman has a third-person narrator, confined to the mind and eyes of the adult Jean Louise. Although the readers know what Jean

Louise thinks, they are not privy to the minds of Atticus and other characters, which are unspoken.

Characterization

Scout and Jean Louise

Both *To Kill a Mockingbird* and *Go Set a Watchman* are character-driven stories. The main focus in both novels is on the relationship between father and daughter, Scout/Jean Louise and Atticus. Scout is bright, feisty, independent, and curious. She is what is described as a tomboy and a daddy's girl. She eschews girlish clothes; her best friends are boys. Even as a child, she seems not to know any little girls. There is no mention of her playing with typical girl playthings like dolls and tea sets. Instead she climbs trees, makes a fort, and plays games with her brother. Neither of her adult female mentors, Miss Maudie and Calpurnia, fit the mold of the Southern belle. She is attracted to those who are different from her and her family, and whom many in her situation would shun—like Boo Radley and Calpurnia. She is open to different experiences, even adventures like approaching Boo, going with Jem to Calpurnia's church, confronting the lynch mob, and sitting with the African Americans in the segregated courtroom.

By the time Jean Louise has grown up in *Go Set a Watchman*, she is no closer to being the Southern belle daughter of a lawyer and legislator. She dresses in pants suits, to the disdain of her Aunt Alexandra, who scolded her about her overalls when she was a child. Her real friends and confidants are not young women like herself, but men, toward one of whom she feels romantic. Her deep, searching conversations are with her Uncle Jack, her boyfriend Henry, and her father. The all-women's party that Aunt Alexandra forces on her angers and disgusts her.

Like the Scout of her youth, she is famous for her unladylike cursing and, as an adult, for her unladylike smoking.

Atticus

Scout/Jean Louise is the voice of both novels, but the most important character in her life and the books is her father, Atticus. Around him the most interest, inspiration, and controversy has raged. More than any character in the two books, Atticus is ruled by his rational, intellectual, educated, practical side. There is little of sentimentality and emotional drama about him. We see that side rarely—when, for example, Scout sends the lynch mob packing and when Tom Robinson is shot to death, and when the minister who is their guest leaves Atticus laughing so hard he is crying. Even when his beloved daughter in *Go Set a Watchman* angrily calls him "a son of a bitch," the response we see is controlled.

Atticus in *To Kill a Mockingbird* is the ideal father. He accepts his motherless children for what they are. Although he threatens them on one occasion when he think they are being hurtful to Boo with their high jinks, he never punishes them, but, like a good attorney, negotiates with them. He encourages their propensities and talents, particularly their love of reading, even in secret defiance of Scout's teacher. He tolerates Scout's unconventional, but benign behavior, like her boyish clothes. He deals kindly but firmly with Dill running away from his relative's house, and he understands his son's traumatic involvement with, and sorrow over, the jury's decision to find Tom Robinson guilty.

Atticus has also been seen by the novel's readers as the model lawyer. He may be ruled by reason, but the reactions to him have often been emotional. Attorneys often point to him as their inspiration to study law. Atticus's character as an attorney in *To Kill a Mockingbird* is formed by his strong moral sense and conscience, neither of which is self-serving. In *Go Set a Watchman*, Atticus, surprisingly, takes on what Jean Louise sees as the less admirable role, in line with the racist community. The change in Atticus's political views from one novel to the other has been a lightning rod for critics.

Jem

Several important characters in *To Kill a Mockingbird* do not appear with Jean Louise and Atticus in *Go Set a Watchman*. Jem, Scout's brother, is the character in *To Kill a Mockingbird* who goes on the most critical journey. Physically he changes in the course of the novel by entering puberty. He is a kind, reflective boy who reads everything he can get his hands on, welcomes the strange neighbor Dill into their company, tolerates his obnoxious younger sister most of the time, makes necessary compromises at school, knows more than the other children about Tom's trial, and seems most affected by Tom's death. Jem, whom Calpurnia adored, has died before the action of *Go Set a Watchman* and his death prompts Calpurnia to leave the family.

Dill

Dill is also a main character in *To Kill a Mockingbird* who has disappeared in *Go Set a Watchman* except in memory. He is physically strange-looking: short for his seven years, with white hair "stuck to his head like duckfluff" (7). His father has deserted the family; his mother has remarried and wants him out of the way. In essence, he has no true home. He is sent for the summer to the home of his great-aunt who lives next door to the Finches. And his acceptance shows that the Finch family is open to people not like themselves. Dill is the imagination incarnate—a reader and movie-goer who is both sharp and sensitive, if eccentric. Like Boo, Dill is a victim, which may be why he is attracted to Boo. Even as a small boy in the balcony of the courtroom, he is so traumatized by the prosecutor's brutal questioning of Tom Robinson that he becomes physically sick and has to be carried out.

Arthur "Boo" Radley

Although he is a focus in the first half and last pages of *To Kill a Mockingbird*, Boo Radley is mostly unseen, a product of the community's and the children's imagination. His parents had been religious fanatics who had nothing to do with their neighbors. When Boo is a young boy and gets into trouble, they bargain to keep him out of industrial school and lock him away in their house for the rest of his days, even when he stabs his father with scissors. After his parents are long dead, his brother keeps him in the house and blocks any attempt of his to have contact with the Finch children, filling up the hole in the tree through which Boo communicates with them. But Boo is capable of laughing at the children, of putting a wrap around Scout in the cold, of folding up Jem's trousers, of carving dolls for them out of soap, of giving them gifts, and of saving the children's lives.

Miss Maudie

Miss Maudie, who lives across the street from the Finches in *To Kill a Mockingbird*, is Scout's support and role model. She is another central character who does not appear in *Go Set a Watchman*. She is single, strong, independent of mind, and dislikes the typical expectations for the appearance and duties of women, characteristics that are obvious and attractive to Scout as a child and Jean Louise as an adult. She stands up to the evangelical churchgoers who scold her from a passing vehicle because of her prideful love of flowers. She also corrects the cruel view of Atticus expressed by a missionary society member. Although Aunt Alexandra is finally grateful for Maudie's defense of her brother, Maudie is the opposite of Aunt Alexandra.

Tom Robinson

Tom Robinson is a doomed and frightened figure whose character is not as fully developed in the first, and only, novel he appears in. We know that he has a wife and children and works hard for a white employer who thinks so much of him that he disrupts the court proceedings from his seat, to object to attacks on Tom's character and to defend him. Tom is a churchgoer. Not only is Tom a decent family man, he is a good man generally, risking sympathy for others, even for those—like Mayella Ewell—who ill-use him. One learns from his testimony that he has regularly, without pay, risked himself by helping her with difficult manual chores. Unfortunately, his expressed kind-heartedness and sympathy for her in the courtroom seals his guilty verdict. How dare a lowly black man feel sorry for a white woman?

There is no clear explanation for Tom's final action, of what impels him to run to the prison fence and fall over it, provoking the guards to shoot him dead. The most fitting word is despair. Atticus's news that Tom's case will be appealed has not allayed Tom's hopelessness and his sense of real possibilities in this community.

Calpurnia

Calpurnia occupies a place often reserved for African American women in the South. She manages the Finch household and rules it with an iron hand. Note that she has a position and exercises authority that would rarely be given by the white professional class to a poor white woman like Mayella Ewell. An argument can be made that she is the strongest person in both novels. Her intelligence and self-education are emphasized in *To Kill a Mockingbird*. She is one of the few African Americans in the community who is able to read, having been taught by her childhood employers.

She must also participate in and balance two distinctly separate cultures. She speaks one "language" in the Finch neighborhood, and as Scout and Jem observe in Calpurnia's church, she speaks a different "language" among people of her own community. The separation of cultures is illustrated by Scout's desire to visit Calpurnia's house, as if it is a fascinating, distinctive world.

She is the Finch children's surrogate mother. The most intense emotional moment in *Go Set a Watchman* is Jean Louise's heart-breaking meeting with Calpurnia, whom she has eagerly sought out, only to learn that Calpurnia now resents the white community (in which she includes Atticus and Jean Louise) and its violent oppression of her people.

The Ewells

The Ewells are only present in *To Kill a Mockingbird*. Mayella Ewell, like Tom Robinson, is a tragic character. Despite her despicable role in trying to tempt Tom and condemn him to death (out of pure terror of her father), she elicits sympathy from Tom and the reader. Like Scout, she is motherless and without female friends—any friends. But Mayella is an inversion of Scout. She is an imprisoned, isolated sex slave of her father. The implication is that she is regularly beaten, raped, and forced, as the eldest child, to take care of the house and the many other children. The one detail in the dark and filthy landscape that puzzles the reader is the bright, carefully tended flowers on Mayella's porch. They suggest a spark of spirit, a heart longing for beauty.

Unlike his daughter, Ewell and his son (who makes a brief disgusting appearance in school) are almost inhuman, lowly personifications of evil. Ewell is the direct opposite of Atticus in his flaunting of the law, his ignorance, his hatred of black people, his disdain for learning, and, most of all, his treatment of his family, especially his daughter. He seems to have no redeeming quality. He lies, slanders, threatens, and sneers at everyone. He condemns Tom, stalks Tom's wife, spits in Atticus's face, and, finally, tries to murder Atticus's children.

Uncle Jack

Atticus's brother, Jack Finch, plays a major role in *To Kill a Mockingbird* and an even larger role in *Go Set a Watchman*. In *To Kill a Mockingbird*, Atticus and his family recognize that Uncle Jack knows nothing about children and, though he flirts with Miss Maudie, has no interest in having a wife and family. An unmarried, bookish doctor, he expresses his disapproval of Scout's manners, dress, and cursing, but comes to see that he has misjudged her. Though they have their differences, Scout knows he is trustworthy when he does not tell Atticus about her cousin Francis's racist taunt.

Jack, now retired and living in Maycomb, is central to *Go Set a Watchman*. He is Jean Louise's confidante and tries to be her mentor, twice, in long conversations, trying to explain Atticus's actions in supporting the White Citizens' Council. At one point he slaps her to bring her to her senses.

Aunt Alexandra

In both novels, Aunt Alexandra, Atticus's sister, represents the values that Scout despises, particularly antebellum Southern ladyhood, classism, and racism, and she fits in perfectly into Maycomb society. She refuses to allow Scout to visit Calpurnia's house in *To Kill a Mockingbird* and scolds her for calling on her in *Go Set a Watchman*. In both novels, she constantly nags Scout about her attire. Chapter 5, on women's issues, delves more deeply into the conflict between Scout and Aunt Alexandra.

Mrs. Dubose

Mrs. Dubose, the vicious, filthy, dying drug addict, is one of the clearest symbolic characters in *To Kill a Mockingbird*, central to a discussion of the South (see chapter 7). A full chapter is devoted to her encounters with Jem, who is made to read to her every day.

Henry Clinton

Henry (or Hank) Clinton is the character introduced in *Go Set a Watchman* as Jean Louise's boyfriend. He is from lower-class whites in the community, has received (a poor) legal education at the state university law school. But he has been trained by Atticus and is likely to take over Atticus's law business when Atticus's health forces him to retire. Henry has ambitions to community leadership as well. He is supposedly in love with Jean Louise and wants her to marry him, against Aunt Alexandra's objections because of his social background but also what she perceives as his ambition. Despite their class differences, he already seems to be a member of the Finch household and, at the beginning of the narrative, Jean Louise regards him as one of her "own kind," a situation that will change when she sees him at Maycomb's Citizens' Council. He defends himself by telling her that since he comes from "trash," he must share the community's values in order to get what he wants: a career, money, and a family.

Structure: *To Kill a Mockingbird*

When *To Kill a Mockingbird* first appeared, some readers criticized it for not being unified, for switching from one distinct plot (involving Boo Radley) to another unrelated plot (Tom Robinson's troubles), and having the narrative thread interrupted by the mad dog and Mrs. Dubose episodes, the last of which was cut from the film. Nevertheless, the novel's dual plots are intertwined, not only with identical characters, but with images and themes of breaking down walls and coming to terms with differences. Atticus's killing of the mad dog is symbolic of his challenge to a mad community and the Dubose chapter lays out the character of that mad community and its obsession with the past.

The Boo Plot

The action of part one of *To Kill a Mockingbird* is devoted to the attempt on the part of the children to make contact with Boo Radley, who has been imprisoned in his house since boyhood. As Jem remembered, the dual drama of their young lives "began the summer Dill came to us, when Dill first gave us the idea of making Boo Radley come out" (3).

Dill leaves at the end of the summer, after which Scout begins suffering from the cruelties of the school that make her feel like a criminal because she can read. In first grade she is also exposed to the class of poor whites, specifically the Cunninghams of Old Sarum, Burris Ewell, and Little Chuck Little. She and Jem also become aware of the devastation of the economic depression.

When Dill returns the following summer, the children begin to dramatize the Radleys' legend, which Atticus puts a stop to. Scout, having begun to realize the unhappy consequences of being a girl, goes to Miss Maudie for comfort. The motive of trying to communicate with Boo begins as they try to pass him a friendly note.

The action accelerates during Dill's last days in Maycomb that second summer, as the children decide to get a look at Boo by approaching his house in the dark. Boo's brother shoots above the cabbage patch to scare off the trespassers and Jem loses his pants scrambling through a fence. Later, in search of his pants, Jem finds them neatly folded.

Scout's irritation with schooling persists in the second grade. Its other major action is the discovery of two carved figures in a knothole of a tree, representing Jem and Scout, a broken watch, and a pocketknife, all, at different times, placed there by Boo. When they try to thank Boo by leaving him a note in the tree, they discover the hole filled in by Boo's brother, a situation that causes Jem to weep.

The Finches' neighbors are introduced in a rare snowstorm when Jem and Scout make a snowman resembling a feminized Mr. Avery, Miss Maudie's house catches on fire, and Boo unobtrusively places a blanket around Scout's shoulders in the cold when she is transfixed by the fire.

Boo returns at the very end of the novel.

The Tom Robinson Plot

The second plot, Atticus's defense of Tom Robinson, is introduced when Scout's classmate Cecil demeans Atticus on the playground. In that same winter Uncle Jack is brought into the novel as a Christmas visitor, along with Aunt Alexandra and her obnoxious son, Francis, whom they are forced to visit in the country. There, outside, after dinner, Scout beats up her cousin for insulting her father with a racial slur.

Chapter 5 belongs to Atticus. It is a turning point in Jem's view of his father when Atticus, because of his former reputation of being a crack marksman (a talent of which the children are unaware), is called upon to shoot a mad dog in the street.

Part Two, beginning the plot devoted to Tom Robinson, starts with the children going to Calpurnia's church where they experience a sole incident of black prejudice against them as whites, but where they are warmly welcomed by the rest of the congregation, and where a collection is taken up for Tom Robinson's family. They come home from church to find Aunt Alexandra waiting for them on the porch. The following chapter is devoted to her initial negative influence on the children's lives.

When Dill returns for the next summer, he hides in the Finch household under a bed. An antagonistic mob gathers in the Finch yard to protest Atticus's defense of Tom, who has been accused of rape. Later, when Atticus disappears at night to go to his office, the children, who are worried, follow him and find him in a chair in front of the jail. Encroaching on him is a mob, including Mr. Cunningham from Old Sarum. Scout disperses the mob with friendly questions to Mr. Cunningham about his little son, who has had lunch at the Finch house, and about his financial problems with which Atticus has helped him.

Chapter 16 begins with the children walking to the courthouse where Tom Robinson is on trial for rape of a young white woman, Mayella Ewell. In the courtyard they observe a white man named Dolphus Raymond, known for his heavy drinking and his choice to live in the black community with a black partner, the mother of his mixed-race children.

Scout, Jem, and Dill, who can't get into the main floor of the courthouse, are invited by Reverend Sykes to sit in the balcony to which black people are relegated. Chapters 17–21 encompass the testimony and the arguments of Tom's trial. Despite the testimony of the Ewells, Atticus is able to prove that Tom, whose left arm is useless from a childhood accident, could not have inflicted wounds on Mayella's face or overcome her. In this section, the children's presence is detected in the balcony by Calpurnia and Atticus, and Tom is found guilty by the jury.

Chapter 24, during the meeting of the missionary society in the Finch house, the appalling traditions of racism and Southern ladyhood come together. The chapter ends with the news of Tom's death.

The novel concludes with illustrations of the blind prejudice in the community, the threatening behavior of Bob Ewell (whom Atticus has humiliated at trial), and Ewell's attack on the children. The final actions return to the first plot when the children are saved by Boo Radley, who carries Jem into the Finch house. The last sentences show Scout escorting Boo home and trying to see the world from his perspective.

Structure: *Go Set a Watchman*

The structure of *Go Set a Watchman* is decidedly at variance with that of *To Kill a Mockingbird*, but it shares the same setting (Maycomb, Alabama), many of the same characters (Jean Louise, Atticus, Calpurnia, Uncle Jack, and Aunt Alexandra), and many of the same issues (those of race and womanhood, for example). Jem and Dill, main characters in *To Kill a Mockingbird*, appear only in memories in *Go Set a Watchman*, and Uncle Jack Finch and Henry (Hank) Clinton become central characters. The Finch house and its neighborhood and neighbors are gone. Significantly fewer characters appear in this novel.

Go Set a Watchman is not driven by physical action. Despite intense conflict, the action here is conversational and reflective, about the grown-up Scout's, Jean Louise's, inner journey through her hometown as she comes to terms with her realization that her father is not an idol and a god, but a flawed human being, particularly because of his ideas on race.

The Return

The story begins with Jean Louise's train trip to Maycomb, one of several returns since her move to New York City. She is about 26 and the year is 1957. Her old boyfriend, Henry (Hank) Clinton, meets her at the station. Matters have remained romantic (even publicly demonstrative) between them, though Jean Louise makes it clear from this ride home that, though she loves him and he is "one of her kind," she will never marry him.

Atticus and his sister, Aunt Alexandra, are waiting for them, and the usual argument arises, and will, repeatedly, between Jean Louise and her aunt over the younger woman's wardrobe.

After the men have departed, Aunt Alexandra pleads (as Uncle Jack will later) for Jean Louise to move back home. Yet her aunt also strenuously argues against a marriage to Henry because, though he is a lawyer and a budding politician, he is, by social rank, "trash."

On a date with Hank that evening, they drive out to the waterway at Finch's Landing where they talk and, at Jean Louise's insistence, jump into the water with their clothes on. The news has already surfaced when she wakes up the next morning, that they had been seen swimming naked the night before.

They all attend church the next day in a chapter that explores past and present differences in religious practices. Back home she discovers a racist book that Atticus has been reading and learns that he and Henry are going to a meeting of Maycomb's Citizens' Council, which astounds her because of a suspicion that it may be a branch of the infamous White Citizens' Council. From Aunt Alexandra, she learns that Atticus is on the board of directors and that Henry is "one of the staunchest members."

The White Citizens' Council

Mortified and puzzled, she follows them and sits in the balcony of the courthouse reserved for black people, where she had once watched her father defend a black man. As memories of the old, compassionate Atticus go through her head, she finds herself listening to the most despicable of racist rants by their guest speaker, Grady O'Hanlon.

After leaving the courthouse, Jean Louise becomes physically sick, throwing up over and over again.

She has memories of her adolescence and then learns of the legal troubles of Calpurnia's grandson, prompting her to visit her old surrogate mother who left the Finch household after Jem died. But Calpurnia is formal and cold to her and questions what Jean Louise's people are doing to black people.

The Coffee Party

Another Maycomb gathering is at a "coffee" given for her by Aunt Alexandra. The guests are young women about Jean Louise's age, mostly newly married or young mothers. She finds them to be dreadfully shallow, boring, limited, mindless, and even racist. The big news that one of the women has to report is that her toddler has a "Crimson Tide" sweatshirt.

She feels driven to search out her Uncle Jack for answers about Atticus's and Henry's behavior, but after a long conversation, she remains unsatisfied with the ironic, literary responses.

The chapter that follows is another memory of young girlhood, ending with Atticus's secretly devised plan to save her and Henry from an embarrassing situation in high school. She explains her recent memories as a reaching out to recapture something lost.

Her next conversation is with Hank in which she decidedly, in the wake of the Maycomb Citizens' Council meeting, again refuses his offer of marriage and listens to his rationalization for being a "staunch" supporter of such a group.

She next confronts Atticus over his views of race, which includes their discussions of the Constitution, states' rights, the NAACP, and voting rights. After he tells her that he loves her despite their differences, she calls him a son-of-a-bitch.

Back at the house, she furiously packs her suitcase to leave immediately and prematurely for her home in New York City, until Uncle Jack appears, slaps her, gives her a drink, and tries again, more successfully, to explain the situation. From this she accepts that she has just come to see reality, having idealized her past and her father. When a veil has been lifted from her eyes, Uncle Jack says she is now her own person, her own conscience, separate from her father.

Still, she is determined that Henry and Maycomb are not for her. The novel ends with her reconciliation with Henry as a friend and, especially, Atticus, welcoming him "silently to the human race."

The Titles

The titles of both novels speak to essential conflicts. As the children in *To Kill a Mockingbird* learn from Atticus and Miss Maudie when they get their rifles from Uncle Jack, it is a sin to harm a helpless, innocent being. Atticus is speaking of the death of the crippled Tom Robinson. Black people are birds whose songs are unheard and whose wings are useless to help them escape. They are treated as children, forced to obey whites (look at Mayella ordering Tom into the yard), and addressed as "boys." Even in *Go Set a Watchman*, Atticus regards black people as children. The concept is introduced by the minister in church, mulled over by Jean Louise, and clarified by Uncle Jack.

Other harmless songbirds are killed, threatened, or silenced in *To Kill a Mockingbird*—not only all the black characters, but Mayella and Arthur Radley. Both Scout and Jean Louise are also birds, attempting to try their wings and songs, but being encaged by a closed, sexist society.

In three instances, the word "Watchman" is used in the story of Jean Louise's confounding return home. In the first, the Reverend Stone refers to the Bible verse containing the word; in the second, after the excruciatingly racist and banal coffee party, she thinks back to Reverend Stone's reading, and thinks that she needs a watchman to explain all the conundrums she is encountering, to tell her the difference between what a person says and what he means, obviously in reference to her father and friend Hank. She needs a watchman to explain to them that she is tired of being misled. Uncle Jack throws some clarity on the symbol of the watchman in his last conversation with her after she has confronted her father.

The "watchman" refers to one's personal conscience: "Every man's island, Jean Louise, every man's watchman, is his conscience. There is no such thing as a collective conscious [sic]" (265). Despite Uncle Jack's observation, longstanding racial bigotry oppresses the conscience itself as basically decent men quietly impede the resistance to racism.

Images and Themes

To Kill a Mockingbird and *Go Set a Watchman* are novels of building awareness. For Scout, it is learning of the failings of her community—a community to which she must be subservient—and learning from walking in the shoes of people she doesn't like or know, ending with trying to see, from the Radley front porch, the world from Mr. Arthur's perspective.

In *Go Set a Watchman* Jean Louise, now a 26-year-old New York City resident, comes back to her "home," Maycomb, the almost ideal nest of her childhood, to discover a greater reality than she has ever faced—not to embrace it but to understand it.

The Gothic Literary Tradition

Both novels, particularly *To Kill a Mockingbird*, are influenced by the gothic literary tradition, or rather a satire of the gothic (very like Jane Austen's *Northanger Abbey* and Mark Twain's *Pudd'nhead Wilson*). Mary Shelley's *Frankenstein*, Bram Stoker's *Dracula* (mentioned in *To Kill a Mockingbird*), and the works of Edgar Allan Poe come to mind. Southern gothic is a particular variant of the genre.

Virtually every external feature of the gothic can be located in the novel, either as part of the action or as an operative element in the children's imaginations.

One: Forebodings of evil;

Two: Ghosts, vampires, witches, and haunted houses;

Three: Sinister secrets;

Four: Insanity;

Five: The baleful Influence of the past and cultural degeneracy;

Six: Eccentricity;

Seven: The lure of terror;

Eight: Imprisonment, barriers, walls, and veils;

Nine: Stereotypes as prisons;

Ten: Protectively good and isolatingly bad taboos including incest, miscegenation, and racial integration;

Eleven: Violence that results in breaking barriers.

The characteristics of the gothic one finds in *To Kill a Mockingbird*, as they have been defined by critics of the form, are: the supernatural (witches, haunted houses, vampires, werewolves, monsters), dysfunctional families, dark secrets, madness and mental decay, a sick obsession with the past and cultural degeneracy, oppressive prisons, walls and the attempt to breach them, the importance of the "Other" (or people or ideas foreign to one's self), incest, rape and other sexual violence, and murder.

The children's imaginations are imbued with aspects of the literary gothic in their love for *Dracula*, their suspicion that Boo is a monster who eats raw squirrels and cats at night, their fascination with the dark secrets hidden in houses like the Radleys' (where they believe a "haint" lives and the pecans are poison), the foreboding of evil in the mad dog in the street, the abnormal Alabama snow, and the witch's house of Mrs. Dubose (that is creepy, smelly, and frightening). Even the courthouse is an ugly symbol of degeneration and ongoing injustice and inequality. There is gothic deformity in the tall antebellum columns attached to the smaller rebuilt postbellum structure, which always struck Scout as dark, filthy, and smelling of urine.

Insanity

Insanity (as in Bram Stoker's *Dracula*, Poe's "The Fall of the House of Usher," and William Faulkner's "A Rose for Emily") is an important gothic theme in *To Kill a Mockingbird*. Boo remains a hermit for his whole life and, in a moment of madness, stabs his father in the leg with scissors for no immediate discernible reason. His whole family seems to be mentally disturbed. Scout and Jem, despite their attraction to Boo, are convinced he is insane. Scout becomes frightened that insects against the screen are Boo's "insane fingers" (55) and Jem concludes, "He's crazy, I reckon, like they say" (72).

Insanity is mentioned in the Finch family, much to Aunt Alexandra's dismay. Cousin Joshua, long ago, was locked up in the mental institution in Tuscaloosa after he tried to kill the university president. Mrs. Dubose is hardly a stable character and "Crazy Addie's" behavior is blamed on Boo.

The most far-reaching insanity is foreshadowed and represented by the mad dog Atticus has to shoot to protect the community: the mad dog is like the whole community, which is overtaken by insanity when faced with the Ewells' charge of a black man's rape of a white woman. It can be seen in the Old Sarum lynch mob, in the crazy trial itself, and the meeting of the missionary society whose members seem to think Tom's wife is somehow implicated in the crime. Atticus confesses to Uncle Jack, "Why reasonable people go stark raving mad when anything involving a Negro comes up, is something I don't pretend to understand" (88).

Obsession with the Past

The gothic obsession with the past is evident in all aspects of life in Maycomb as its citizens don't seem to be able to let go the Civil War and racism, an idea that will be examined more closely in chapter 7 on the South.

Walls

As poet Robert Frost wrote, "Something there is that does not love a wall." The central gothic theme and image that runs through both novels is the idea of stifling barriers, prisons—walls. Many literal walls pose threats to characters: the imprisoning walls of the Radley house that Boo never leaves and the jail Boo is threatened with as a boy. The boy Arthur Radley and his wild friends seem to have found the town of Maycomb itself and his family's religion to be a prison. He is threatened with the mental institution where Scout's poetic relative died years ago.

The most gothic episode in the novel is Dill's imaginative story of having been bound by chains and left in the cellar of his house to die. There he says a farmer who heard his cries for help saves his life by pushing a bushel of peas, pod by pod, through the ventilator, and Dill frees himself by pulling the chains from the wall. Still in chains, he joins an animal show and travels with them, washing the camels, until they reach within walking distance of Maycomb.

Other gothic walls include the jail where Tom is incarcerated and the fence he scrambles over when he is shot. The jail is symbolic of the racist community itself, filled with incarcerated black men. There is the forbidding wall of Mrs. Dubose's witch house, the house where Mayella is confined, and the hated school where Scout is scolded for having learned to read too soon.

Imprisoning Stereotypes

Cruel stereotypes of race, gender, class, and culture are the stones in this wall that Jean Louise Finch calls the South of the 1930s and the

1950s. The wisdom and humanity of any given characters are shown in the degree to which they see others not as types, but as multidimensional human beings.

All black people are stereotyped in both novels as being irresponsible, uncivilized children, being denied full humanity. Lower-class citizens, including those of Old Sarum, are generally stereotyped as immoral and lazy, a view that is challenged in Scout's mind by Mayella's love and care of her flowers and Mr. Cunningham's pride in not accruing debt. Scout and Jean Louise suffer from the burdens of stereotyping in a different way: they refuse to assume the view of typical females.

The children's stereotyping of their neighbor is seen in their renaming him Boo, burdening him with all the characteristics they have picked up from gothic literature. At the end of *To Kill a Mockingbird* there is evidence that Boo has gotten rid of some stones of stereotype when he appears in person, Scout now addressing him respectfully as "Mr. Arthur." In doing this, she moves him outside the realm of the gothic.

Dysfunctional Families

A characteristic of the gothic that is part of *To Kill a Mockingbird* is a family so dysfunctional that it becomes a site of horror and terror. The Radleys and the Ewells fall into this category. The Radleys sacrifice the life of Boo on the altar of religious fanaticism. Mayella is psychologically mutilated by the twisted cruelty of her father. The main gothic taboo under this topic is incest, usually presented by 19th-century writers like Edgar Allan Poe and Herman Melville as sex between brother and sister. The most horrendous evidence of gothic incest is Mayella's rape by her father. Atticus even refers to the intermarriage of their ancestors (much to Aunt Alexandra's displeasure) as incest. Less balefully, the arrival of Aunt Alexandra throws the Finch household off balance with demands and quarrels. Dill's childhood is ruined by the desertion of his father and his mother's remarriage.

The Gothic and Reality

In what is basically a realistic novel, gothic elements of abnormality shape the action. Peculiar moments (like the unseasonable snow) intrude on reality and, as critics point out, the case is made that the world is not made up of the so-called realism seen by most people. Another view is that the realism we think we see is just on the surface; the truth is just beneath the surface. Finally, maybe there is no "reality" at all—just our fictions. *To Kill a Mockingbird* includes all these elements to various degrees.

A kind of magic prevails in Boo's sense of the children and their needs and his ability to save them. Bob Ewell's essence is so monstrously evil that it seems to come from some place beneath reality. Sometimes the story seems to suggest that what is real is perspective, like the children's vision of Boo and the trial. Then the establishment in the novel thinks it knows the reality of black people and their lives whereas we see evidence that their assumptions are simply not true. The reader is led to ask, is society's version of reality less true than the children's view? Or the author's?

Although it would seem that the horrors of Bob Ewell's malice and Tom's fate would classify the novel as unromantic, it relates to some aspects of Edgar Allan Poe's philosophy. Poe, classified as both a romantic and a gothic writer, believed, like the Transcendentalists, that the truth lay beneath the surface of the world, or in a spiritual world, and that sometimes a deep feeling of horror was the way to reach the truth. The children of *To Kill a Mockingbird* differ from Poe's gothic stories in that from the depths of horror they awaken to a wholeness of vision.

The "Other"

The discussion of the gothic leads to a major theme of *To Kill a Mockingbird*, which is turned on its head in *Go Set a Watchman*: one's attraction to and fear of persons and things and ideas which are different from one's own, the "not-self," as critic William Patrick Day calls it. Day defines the true gothic as the fear *and desire* that the barrier between the self and the Other will be broken. This includes such literary characters as Frankenstein's monster and Count Dracula. The penultimate Other in *To Kill a Mockingbird* is Boo and black people in the community; in *Go Set a Watchman*, the animalistic creature on the cover of Atticus's book is the ultimate Other.

In *To Kill a Mockingbird* and *Go Set a Watchman* both, the idea that directs every community action is that the wall between blacks and whites will be broken by sexual union of the races. This puts the Other behind the discriminatory wall called segregation, a social and legal idea so important in *Go Set a Watchman*.

A satiric treatment of the theme of difference occurs with Aunt Alexandra's missionary society, largely devoted to the "saving" of people who could scarcely be more different—the Mrunas, whom they do not consider fully human. The Mrunas live a safe distance away so that they pose no threat that the ladies will ever have to interact with them. Still, they are without question almost sexually drawn to talk about the "sin and squalor" of the dark Mrunas, morbidly fascinated with what they have heard of the Mrunas' puberty rituals and their bark-chewing-induced psychedelic states.

Mayella's attraction to the dark difference she sees in Tom Robinson leads to the rape trial. Tom attests to her calling him into her yard repeatedly to do chores: "She'd call me in, suh. Seemed like every time I passed by yonder she'd have some little somethin' for me to do" (191). Mayella feels a sexual attraction to Tom: "She reached up an' kissed me 'side of the face" (194).

Atticus encourages dealing with the Other intellectually as he tells the children to "climb into his skin and walk around in it," speaking of people with whom they are having difficulty, including Bob Ewell.

The children's fear of and attraction to Boo is illustrative of this definition. Their desire to see, to contact this unknown fearful Other becomes an obsession, the center of their lives. They embrace him when he leaves articles for them in the tree. There is a twist of the Dracula story in the novel in that Boo, the monster of their own making, becomes transformed first into the familiar and, later, their guardian angel, a savior. It is Boo, the Other, whom they have both feared and longed to know, who saves their lives.

Psychologically, *To Kill a Mockingbird* illustrates the idea, developed by philosophers like Jacques Lacan, that in encountering alien entities within our world (and within ourselves) we break boundaries that imprison us and sometimes embrace a larger world. While Arthur Radley—the unknown Other whom they fear and are attracted to— dominates the opening chapters of the novel, a black man's story dominates the plot that follows. What the reader discovers is what the children discover—that their imaginatively constructed world of dark secrets and evil spirits pales beside the real world underneath the surface, containing more evil than they could have possibly encountered supernaturally. The Other emerges, especially for Scout, in the African American characters in the novel, as she finds, after attending church with Calpurnia, that while African Americans have been a comforting, familiar, and integral part of her life, they are totally separate and unknown to her. Still, in the context of Tom's trial, the children easily and completely identify with the black citizens of Maycomb, literally and symbolically breaking the boundaries that separate them to sit in the balcony and witness the trial with the same sympathies as those who surround them.

For Jem, who at the time of Tom's trial has reached young manhood, the encounters with differences—Tom, Mayella, Bob Ewell, Mrs. Dubose—comprise a kind of mythical rite of passage. The attack on Jem at the end will leave him with an injured arm, a less serious wound than Tom's paralyzed arm.

Courage

Basic to their encounter with difference is courage, one of the many evidences of civilization in the novel. Courage in *To Kill a Mockingbird* is defined as the intellectual ability to overcome base fears of the flesh. The symbol of bravery is Atticus, the man who confronts a mad dog in the streets, who stops to chat with the hateful Mrs. Dubose ("It was at times like these when I thought my father, who hated guns and had never been to any wars, was the bravest man who ever lived" [100]).

The children summon up courage to come to terms with the ghostly mystery of the Radley house: Jem is brave in touching the Radley house, in trying to peep in the window of the house, and in going back to get his pants that got stuck on a wire fence when Mr. Radley was shooting at him. Scout bravely takes part in the Radley dramas even though only she is sure that Boo is alive because she has heard him laugh. At one point, she taunts Jem: "Anybody who's brave enough to go up and touch the house hadn't oughta use a fishing pole."

The subject of courage comes up in Atticus's description of Mrs. Dubose, who makes up her mind to die free from her addiction to morphine. The children's father tells them, "I wanted you to see what real courage is, instead of getting the idea that courage is a man with a gun in his hand. . . . She was the bravest person I ever knew" (112).

Chaos and the Breaking of Barriers

The breaking of barriers, while it may result in unity and wisdom, almost always results in some kind of chaos, disruption. One such occasion is Scout's teacher's meeting across class lines with Burris Ewell, which results in bringing her to horrified tears and Burris yelling at her that "Ain't no snot-nosed slut of a schoolteacher ever born c'n make me do nothin'" (20). Another disturbance happens when Scout's classmate Walter Cunningham of Old Sarum visits the Finch's household. He disrupts the lunch by pouring syrup over his vegetables and meat, triggering Scout to make rude remarks for which Calpurnia scolds her. Radley fires his rifle at Jem when he approaches the back porch of the Radley house.

An unpleasant conflict occurs when the white children attend Calpurnia's black church. Lula, one of the church members, tells Calpurnia, "You ain't got no business bringin' white chillun here—they got their church, we got our'n. It is our church, ain't it, Miss Cal?" The most perilous crossing of boundaries is Tom's going through the door of the Ewell house.

In *Go Set a Watchman* the gothic theme takes a different turn. Jean Louise often mentioned "my own kind" but comes to see that her childhood community, including her boyfriend and her father, are not her own kind. She belongs outside the wall surrounding Maycomb. Her home is in New York, the U.S. city most opposite of Maycomb. It is the ogre and witches of the White Citizens' Council and the coffee party who become the monstrous Others. Finally, in Maycomb she sees no family, no home—just difference surrounding her, not a one "of her kind."

Legal Walls

Gothic walls are of many kinds—those that imprison behind stereotyping and segregation, those that one breaks through with the result of chaos, those that lock people in, but there are also walls that protect. Laws, like the United States Constitution, are intended to protect individuals, to offer order and justice. The subject of laws and legalities pervades *To Kill a Mockingbird*. The novel begins with a line from Charles Lamb: "Lawyers, I suppose, were children once," referring to the innocence that the lawyer grows out of, just as the children's innocence is challenged. The lines reference Jem who already is able to follow with greater interest and acumen than most adults the nuances of a trial that is the central event of the novel. They also make reference to the missionary society's cruel teasing of Scout, as planning to be a lawyer because she attended the trial. Of particular importance here is that the novel's hero is a lawyer.

Formal and informal legalities run throughout the novel: Maycomb's "primary reason for existence was government" (131); entailments (Mr. Cunningham), informal agreements (between Scout and Atticus over school and the reading her teacher has forbidden her to do), state legislative bills introduced by Atticus, treaties (between the Finch children and Miss Maudie over her azaleas), truancy laws that the poor, working children are allowed to break, hunting and trapping laws that the poor, especially Bob Ewell, are allowed to break, and even ignoring the law at the end when there is no investigation into Ewell's death.

That laws are both good and bad barriers in the novel is shown by Scout herself who is seen as an outlaw by the ladies of the community and by Aunt Alexandra because she doesn't follow the rules of the proper little girl and is being raised by her father and a black woman. As early as first grade she discovers her true lawlessness when her teacher admonishes her for knowing how to read. She drags home, "weary from the day's crimes" (29). As a result of her teacher's scolding she wallows "illicitly in the daily papers" (17).

Others in the novel resist either good or bad community codes: the Radleys; Miss Maudie (with her excessive love of flowers); Mrs. Dubose, a morphine addict; Dolphus Raymond living with black people; Tom Robinson, by feeling sorry for a white woman; and Bob Ewell, completely lawless on every possible level.

When laws and social codes conflict, the law is ignored in this community. Tom Robinson's trial is the main example.

Atticus in *To Kill a Mockingbird*, presenting a closing argument in defense of Tom, tries to convince the jury by invoking the legal code of the United States.

> There is one way in this country in which all men are created equal— there is one institution that makes a pauper equal of a Rockefeller, the stupid man the equal of an Einstein, and the ignorant man the equal of any college president. That institution, gentlemen, is a court. It can be the Supreme Court of the United States or the humblest J.P. court in the land, or this honorable court which you serve. Our courts have their faults, as does any human institution, but in this country of ours courts are the great levelers, and in our courts all men are created equal. (205)

But even in this moment, Atticus realizes that the law of this United States is in conflict with what he calls "the secret courts of men's hearts" (241). The last is what the community and the juries live by, not necessarily what they profess.

Jem and Atticus's later discussion sheds light on the effect that the region's tribal system has on juries. With black people walled off from voting and, thus, juries, as in the Scottsboro trials occurring at the same time, they are legally walled off from justice. On April 4, 1935, the *Montgomery Advertiser*, in the same year as Tom's trial, published an editorial acknowledging the dual system of justice in which women and black people are not excluded legally, but "in common practice they are, of course."

From these literary and psychological themes, symbols, and structure, we now move to social issues.

Further Reading

Bloom, Harold, ed. *To Kill a Mockingbird: Modern Critical Interpretations*. Philadelphia: Chelsea House Books, 1999.

Dave, R. A. "*To Kill a Mockingbird*: Harper Lee's Tragic Vision." In *Indian Studies in American Fiction*, edited by M. K. Naik, S. K. Desai, and S. Mokashi-Punekar, 26–30. Dharwar: Karnatak University and the Macmillan Company of India, 1974.

Day, William Patrick. *In the Circles of Fear and Desire: A Study of Gothic Fantasy*. Chicago: University of Chicago Press, 1985.

Erisman, Fred. "The Romantic Regionalism of Harper Lee." *Alabama Review* (1973): 122–36.

Going, William. "Store and Mockingbird: Two Pulitzer Novels about Alabama." In *Essays on Alabama Literature*, 9–13. Tuscaloosa: University of Alabama Press, 1975.

Gopnik, Adam. "Harper Lee's Failed Novel about Race." *New Yorker*, July 27, 2015. https://www.newyorker.com/magazine/2015/07/27/sweet-home-alabama.

Hoff, Timothy. "Influences on Harper Lee: An Introduction to the Symposium." *Alabama Law Review* 45 (Winter 1994): 389.

Johnson, Claudia Durst. "The Secret Courts of Men's Hearts: Code and Law in Harper Lee's *To Kill a Mockingbird*." *Studies in American Fiction* 19 (Autumn 1991): 129–39.

Johnson, Claudia Durst. *To Kill a Mockingbird: Threatening Boundaries*. New York: Twayne Publishers, 1994.

Johnson, Claudia Durst. *Understanding "To Kill a Mockingbird": A Student Casebook to Issues, Sources, and Historical Documents*. Westport, CT: Greenwood Press, 1994.

Keller, Julia. "Review: *Go Set a Watchman* by Harper Lee." *Chicago Tribune*, July 20, 2017. http://www.chicagotribune.com/lifestyles/books/ct-prj-go-set-a-watchman-harper-lee-20150710-story.html.

Kennedy, Randall. "Harper Lee's *Go Set a Watchman*." *New York Times*, July 14, 2015. https://www.nytimes.com/2015/07/14/books/review/harper-lees-go-set-a-watchman.html?_r=0.

Lawson, Mark. "*Go Set a Watchman* Review." *The Guardian*, May 13, 2015. https://www.theguardian.com/books/2015/jul/12/go-set-a-watchman-review-harper-lee-to-kill-a-mockingbird.

Lee, Harper. *Go Set a Watchman*. New York: HarperCollins, 2015.

Lee, Harper. *To Kill a Mockingbird*. Philadelphia: J. B. Lippincott, 1960. Warner Books paperback edition, 1982.

O'Neill, Terry, ed. *Readings on "To Kill a Mockingbird"*. San Diego: Greenhaven Press, 2000.

Ragland-Sullivan, Ellie. *Jacques Lacan and the Philosophy of Psychoanalysis.* Urbana: University of Illinois Press, 1986.

Rubin, Louis D., Jr., et al., eds. *A History of Southern Literature.* Baton Rouge: Louisiana State University Press, 1985.

Stuckey, W. J. *The Pulitzer Prize Novels: A Critical Backward Look.* Norman: University of Oklahoma Press, 1981.

CHAPTER FOUR

Race Relations in Harper Lee's Works

The barrier that walls off blacks from basic rights and opportunities and from the dominant white culture is a central focus of *To Kill a Mockingbird* and *Go Set a Watchman*, both narrated by Southerners, the first from an innocent child's point of view, and the second from a young adult's "colorblind" point of view.

To Kill a Mockingbird: 1930s in Maycomb, Alabama

In *To Kill a Mockingbird*, the racial theme is seen in multiple phases: the children's relationship with Calpurnia; the racial attitudes and racial slurs of the extended family, school, neighborhood, and community when Atticus takes Tom Robinson's case; the attempted lynching; the Ewells' charge and the trial itself; and Aunt Alexandra's missionary society.

Calpurnia: Black Woman as Surrogate Mother

In the 1930s community of Maycomb, the line between the races is accurately and rigidly delineated, the irony being that, as in so many white households, a black woman, in this case Calpurnia, is the surrogate mother to the white children of a widower. In other cases, sometimes the white mother worked; sometimes her social life took up all her time. Like many other maids, Calpurnia is a loving mother of both her own and her surrogate children. One of the few black people who can read in Maycomb is the garbage man, Zeebo, Calpurnia's son. "There wasn't a school even when he was a boy," so she taught him. And Calpurnia also teaches Scout to write long before she reaches first grade.

Atticus trusts Calpurnia to take over important parental duties, including discipline, to the point that the six-year-old Scout complains about her sometimes as a tyrannical presence. An outstanding instance is when Scout makes fun of their guest, Walter Cunningham, from a poor family. Calpurnia pulls her into the kitchen immediately: "That boy's yo comp'ny and if he wants to eat up the table cloth you let him, you hear?" (24). When Scout complains to Atticus about Calpurnia and how she favors Jem, he strongly reinforces whatever this black woman does and says: "You think about how much Cal does for you, and you mind her, you hear" (25).

In first grade, Scout's irritable relationship with Calpurnia changes as Cal is no longer so critical and Scout tries not to do things to provoke her. When Jem is twelve and he and Scout begin quarreling more often, Scout turns to the other woman in the house, Calpurnia, as a confidante: "She seemed glad to see me when I appeared in the kitchen" (115) and Calpurnia tries to explain Jem's adolescence to her.

The wall of race blocks Calpurnia even in the relatively compassionate Finch household, even before Aunt Alexandra's arrival. When Atticus has to go to Montgomery periodically to serve in the legislature, Calpurnia must stay overnight in the house to care for Jem and Scout, but, despite the empty (Atticus's) bedroom, Calpurnia must sleep on a cot in the kitchen.

One of the most segregated arenas in the South were the white churches. Even as late as the 1970s, blacks were forbidden from entering most Protestant churches. Except for one contentious woman, Jem and Scout are welcomed by all into Calpurnia's church. They see another side of Calpurnia—another of her lives—when they visit her church. She speaks another language and she defends them against the antagonistic Lula, a fellow church member. It is this experience that causes Scout to want to know more about Calpurnia, reflecting on how Calpurnia had been taught to read by Miss Maudie's aunt and how she had taught Zeebo to read from "Blackstone's *Commentaries*." "That Calpurnia led a modest double life never dawned on me" (125). At this point, Scout, with her attraction to Calpurnia, wants to know more about her by visiting in her home. "I was curious, interested; I wanted to be her 'company,' to see how she lived, who her friends were" (224).

Her plan is thwarted when, right after the church service, a true racist moves into their home, trying unsuccessfully to take over Calpurnia's role as surrogate mother. In a defense of Calpurnia, whom Aunt Alexandra wants out of their lives, Atticus stands his ground: "Alexandra, Calpurnia's not leaving this house until she wants to. You may think otherwise, but I couldn't have gotten along without her all these years. She's a faithful member of this family. . . . She tried to bring them up according to her lights, and Cal's lights are pretty good—and another thing, the children love her" (137).

Tom Robinson and Dolphus Raymond: The Wall between Blacks and Whites

The disaster that forms the core of *To Kill a Mockingbird* arises from a particular kind of wall: the wall white Southerners thought they had to erect to protect their daughters from what they were convinced were lecherous black males. (This was actually given later, in *Go Set a Watchman*, as the reason to keep schools racially segregated.) The wall is represented by the Ewells' front door. Once Tom crosses that boundary, at Mayella's insistence, in order, he believes, to help her, he opens himself to the Ewells' false charge of rape and dooms himself to death.

Scout, Dill, and Jem also cross the wall between the races when they watch the trial in the balcony of the courthouse, to which blacks are relegated. They become one with the black people when they stand with them at the end of the trial in reverence to Atticus: "Miss Jean Louise, stand up. Your father's passin'" (211).

The children are fascinated by a case in which the barrier, so rigidly maintained by the white community, has been broken. This is in the person of Dolphus Raymond and his mixed-race children, whom they encounter at Tom Robinson's trial. The black people, among the crowds gathering for the trial, are alone in a group, as if a fence surrounded them. The one white person with them is Dolphus Raymond, who has partnered with a black woman, had children by her, and lives among black people. What he has done is so disgusting to white Maycomb that, as he tells Dill, he refuses to dispel the general rumor that he is drunk all the time, to give the townspeople an excuse for his behavior: "I try to give 'em a reason, you see. It helps folks if they can latch onto a reason. . . . but you see they could never, never understand that I live like I do because that's the way I want to live" (201).

After their discussion about Dolphus Raymond and his children, Scout raises the question: "Well, how do we know we ain't Negroes?" Jem gives an answer that would have caused the snooty, ancestor-conscious Aunt Alexandra to keel over: "Uncle Jack Finch says we really don't know. He says as far as he can trace back the Finches we ain't, but for all he knows we mighta come straight out of Ethiopia durin' the Old Testament. . . .

around here once you have a drop of Negro blood, that makes you all black."

Atticus: A Voice for Racial Justice

The racism in the community is apparent in the community's hatred of Atticus—not because he agrees to represent a black man but because he makes clear that he intends to truly defend him. The children hear men talking about their father in the courtyard:

> "Lemme tell you somethin' now, Billy," a third said, "you know the court appointed him. . . ."
> "Yeah, but Atticus aims to defend him. That's what I don't like about it."
> (163)

The hatred, usually expressed in a racial slur, is shown by the towns-people, the neighbors, the schoolchildren, the people on the courthouse lawn, and even Atticus's own sister and her family. At school Scout hears constant racial slurs against her father but has promised him that she won't get into a fistfight about it. Francis, Aunt Alexandra's grandson who is about her age, tells Scout that Atticus's actions "mortify the rest of the family" and that Aunt Alexandra tells him that "we'll never be able to walk the streets of Maycomb agin. He's ruinin' the family, that's what he's doin'" (83). Scout hears her Aunt Alexandra continually attacking Atticus about Tom's trial after she moves in. Aunt Alexandra "won't let him alone about Tom Robinson. She almost said Atticus was disgracin' the family" (147). The children hear racist comments about Atticus on the downtown street. Men who know they are "some Finches," say in front of the chil-dren: "They c'n go loose and rape up the countryside for all 'em who run this country care." And, of course, Mrs. Dubose flings racial epithets at the children every time they have to walk by her house.

It is not just the Old Sarum crowd who are furious at Atticus. Among the crowd who approach the Finch house to protest his actions are "peo-ple we saw everyday: merchants, in-town farmers; Dr. Reynolds was there; so was Mr. Avery" (134).

The hatred that Jem senses is so intense that he fears for his father's life. He feels that the crowd who enter their yard before the trial are out to get Atticus for defending Tom even though Atticus says naively that there is nothing to worry about because the men are "our friends." Jem suspects that the KKK is behind the danger he feels, but again Atticus dismisses the Klan as a joke. "It's gone," he says, "It'll never come back" (147). Still,

Jem's alarm is not assuaged, and he tells Scout afterward that he is afraid for Atticus: "Somebody might hurt him" (147).

The next night, everyone's fear is justified as a drunken Old Sarum group arrives at the front of the jail with the intent of forcing Atticus to hand Tom over to them to be lynched.

The Trial: Black People Walled Off from Justice

The arrest, jailing, trial, and conviction of Tom Robinson are evidence of another symbolic wall that surrounds the black community: they are walled off from justice. In the courtroom, Tom is surrounded by white people but not justice. As in the Scottsboro trials, Tom is not judged by a jury of his peers. In fact, in Tom's case, not only are there no black people on the jury, but the body is made up of his worst enemies, the residents of Old Sarum, the very people who planned to lynch him before the case got to trial. Scout already knows something about juries, that these sun-burned, lanky men dressed in overalls were likely all farmers because townspeople rarely sat on juries. They remind her of the lynch mob and the smell of whiskey from that night comes back to her.

As in the Scottsboro trial, irrefutable evidence has no effect on the racial prejudice of the jury or most of the town's citizens. Ewell's language during his testimony is deliberately racist and obscene, so obscene that the judge orders women and children to leave the courtroom and the Reverend thinks that the children, especially Scout, should leave.

Although the black enclave near Ewell's house is pristine, especially compared with his own pigpen of a house, he takes this opportunity to rail against the county leaders who have failed to "clean out" his black neighbors, as he has asked them to do. The prosecutor's cross-examination of Tom makes Dill so physically sick that the children have to leave the courtroom. "It ain't right, somehow it ain't right to do 'em that way. Hasn't anybody got any business talkin' like that—it just makes me sick" (199).

Atticus's closing argument speaks to the matter of race and the racist code that governs the community and denies black people justice and basic human rights. Speaking of Mayella, he argues, she has put "a man's life at stake, which she has done in an effort to get rid of her own guilt. . . . I say guilt, gentlemen, because it was guilt that motivated her. She has committed no crime, she has merely broken a rigid and time-honored code of our society, a code so severe that whoever breaks it is hounded from our midst as unfit to live with. . . . What did she do? She tempted a Negro."

Despite the ample evidence that Tom could not have hit Mayella on that side of her face or choked her around her whole neck or raped her because of his useless arm, and the proven lies of his accusers, the jury finds him guilty.

After the verdict, Atticus gives his own opinion: "There is something in our world that makes men lose their heads—they couldn't be fair if they tried. In our courts, when it's a white man's word against a black man's, the white man always wins" (220). He also tells his children that they will see white men cheat black men "every day of your life."

After the Trial: Racism Continues

After the trial is over and Atticus is preparing to mount an appeal, as lawyers had done in the Scottsboro trials, the racism in the community is now even more transparent, again, not just in the poorer sections of the county, but in the middle and upper ranks of religious white women, as one sees at Aunt Alexandra's missionary society gathering. The heartless irony is that while the society focuses on "saving" the Mrunas in Africa, they deny black Americans, who live in their midst, basic necessities and human rights. What is even more disturbing is that they curse Tom Robinson's wife, though she has had nothing to do with the scenario that left Tom imprisoned. She is saved by Tom's old boss who gives her a job and tries to protect her from Bob Ewell, who begins stalking her.

The missionary women also charge their black servants with being difficult and moody because of the trial. Mrs. Farrow, who has a speech impediment, expresses the view of most of her friends: "'S-s-s Grace,' she said, 'it's just like I was telling Brother Hutson the other day. S-s-s Brother Hutson,' I said, 'looks like we're fighting a losing battle, a losing battle.' I said, 'S-s-s it doesn't matter to 'em one bit. We can educate 'em til we're blue in the face, we can try til we drop to make Christians out of 'em, but there's no lady safe in her bed these nights.'" (232). Then Mrs. Merriweather lights into Atticus without mentioning his name—"good but misguided people . . . and all they did was stir 'em [black people] up." At this point Miss Maudie steps in to defend Atticus and they change the topic.

Later, Scout talks about the hypocrisy and racism of her teacher, Miss Gates, who rails against Hitler in the classroom. She touts DEMOCRACY and approves of Scout's definition: "Equal rights for all, special privileges for none" (245). But Scout is confused because she has heard the words of her teacher about black people outside the courtroom: "I heard her say it's time somebody taught 'em a lesson, they were gettin' way above themselves, an' next thing they think they can do is marry us. Jem, how can you hate Hitler so bad an' then turn around and be ugly about folks right at home?" (247).

Mr. B. B. Underwood, the editor of the newspaper and no lover of black people, in an editorial connects the title and theme of the novel to the innocent Tom's death. "He likened Tom's death to the senseless slaughter of songbirds" (241).

Maycomb is interested in Tom's death for about two days and manages to treat it as the typical cowardly behavior expected of a black man: typical of him to cut and run, to have "no plan, no thought for the future, just run blind first chance he saw. . . . You know how they are. Easy come, easy go. Just shows you, the Robinson boy was legally married, they say he kept himself clean, went to church and all that, but when it comes down to the line the veneer's mighty thin" (240).

The Problem of the "N" Word

To Kill a Mockingbird has been frequently challenged in public schools because of the use of the "N" word. It is important to note that Atticus never uses the word himself and that he scolds Scout for using it because it is "common" to do so. They discuss it again after she hears Mrs. Dubose using the language in reference to Atticus's defense of a black man. Looking back to his 1930s view, one has to acknowledge his naiveté in his explanation: "just one of those terms that don't mean anything—like snot-nose. It's hard to explain—ignorant, trashy people use it when they think somebody's favoring Negroes over and above themselves" (108).

Yet the objection on the part of many readers is that there is frequent use of the "N" word throughout the novel, as there is, for example, in *Huckleberry Finn*. A counter-argument to this objection is that omitting the word from the novel results in "prettying up" the language of bigots, so, to be realistic about the racist culture of a book on racism, the word has to be on the lips of certain characters in the novel.

One note here about the "N" word and the teaching of the novel. There is no necessity to speak or read it aloud in the classroom. In fact, it should *not* be spoken because it is extremely painful to students (even to those who might deny that it is). It is cruel for teachers to insist on speaking, or worse, having it read out loud by students, to prove some unnecessary point.

Go Set a Watchman: Race in 1950s Maycomb, Alabama

Civil rights with respect to race is the central conversation in *Go Set a Watchman,* from which other matters like the issues of women, family,

Southern culture, and heroism flow. The setting is about 1957, over 20 years after Tom Robinson's trial, in the same town of Maycomb, Alabama. Relations between blacks and whites in Maycomb have become much more openly contentious as black people have become increasingly vocal about the injustice of their situation, especially in the South.

Jean Louise has been reared in Maycomb, but in New York she has been removed (or has removed herself) from the political scene that engrosses its citizens in the 1950s. She and Hank and Atticus begin talking politics as soon as she arrives in the house. When Hank and Atticus ask her about what she knows of politics in the South, she says she reads about Governor Jim Folsom's sexual indiscretions in the tabloids, the violence following the Montgomery bus strikes, and "the Mississippi business," probably referring to the lynching of Emmett Till. She goes on to say that "the state's not getting a conviction in that case was our worst blunder since Pickett's Charge" (24). On this she and Atticus agree.

But attention turns to the activities of the NAACP. Jean Louise seems to have little knowledge of the organization but has placed the Christmas seals they sent her on all her cards. Atticus and Hank soon reveal that they consider the organization as disruptive and dangerous. The first mention of the United States Supreme Court recent activity, especially in deciding *Brown v. Board of Education* and, as the family sees it, violating states' rights to ensure school integration, comes when Uncle Jack complains about the way the singing of familiar hymns has been changed: "apparently our brethren in the Northland are not content merely with the Supreme Court's activities. They are now trying to change our hymns on us" (97).

Jean Louise's Devastating Discovery: The White Citizens' Council

The trigger for the racial theme in the novel is Jean Louise's discovery in the living room, after her father has left the house, of a pamphlet he has been reading. On the cover is the picture of an "anthropophageous [or man-eating] Negro" (101). The title is *The Black Plague*. In bitter sarcasm, she summarizes the pamphlet for her aunt: "I especially liked the part where the Negroes, bless their hearts, couldn't help being inferior to the white race because their skulls are thicker and their brain-pans shallower—whatever that means—so we must all be very kind to them and not let them do anything to hurt themselves and keep them in their places. Good God, Aunty—" (102).

Aunt Alexandra is in perfect agreement with the pamphlet. Jean Louise, in spite of her aunt's objections, furiously throws it in the garbage.

The discovery of the pamphlet impels her to ask about the meeting Atticus and Hank have left to attend.

She is shocked to learn that the young man, whom she had assumed was "one of her kind" and whom she loves, and the father she has idolized have gone to a White Citizens' Council meeting in the courthouse where, incongruously, Atticus had defended a black man so many years ago. Not only are they attending, she is told, but Atticus is on the board of directors and Henry is "one of its staunchest members." Recognizing Jean Louise's horror, Aunt Alexandra tells her, "I don't think you fully realize what's been going on down here" (103).

As it turns out, Jean Louise knew of these "councils" from cursory reading in New York City and characterizes them as being little more than more "respectable" Klan members: "same people who were the Invisible Empire, who hated Catholics; ignorant, fear-ridden, red-faced, boorish law-abiding one hundred per cent red-blooded Anglo-Saxons, her fellow Americans—trash" (104).

Despite all her aunt has told her and her finding of the pamphlet, she still can't quite believe Atticus would be involved. In doubt and distress, she walks to the courthouse and sits in the same "Colored" balcony from which she viewed Atticus's defense of Tom Robinson.

Below her in the courtroom are seated not only what she knows to be the lower-class men of the community, but the most respectable men, and the notoriously crooked business and professional leaders. Most distressing of all she observes that Henry and Atticus occupy places of importance in this group and Atticus introduces the nauseatingly racist speaker.

What she hears from their guest speaker, Grady O'Hanlon, wipes out any hope that this group is any better than the ones she has read about in the papers: "marry your daughters . . . mongrelize the race . . . lower than cockroaches . . . save the South . . . nobody knows why but He intended for 'em to stay apart . . . if He hadn't He'd've made us all one color" (108).

As the speech goes on, Jean Louise remembers her father's defense in this same courtroom of a black man charged with rape. It was a case that had come to him from Calpurnia and he had taken it because he was convinced that the accused man was innocent of the charges.

Then she returns from her memories back to the racist speech being given in the same courtroom so many years later. The speaker contends that Christian civilization is being challenged and blames Communists who have made blacks their slaves, the Jews who killed Jesus, and Mrs. Roosevelt.

The uncritical looks on the faces of Atticus and especially Hank during this speech make her physically sick. As if this experience weren't bad enough, the conversations she has soon after with Hank and Atticus confirm their racism.

The NAACP and Calpurnia

When a white drunk staggers out in front of Zeebo's son's car and is killed, Atticus takes the case. For a moment, Jean Louise still has hope that Atticus does not concur with the view of the White Citizens' Council, that his love for their black family—Calpurnia and Zeebo—still prevails. After Hank reports that he has told the sheriff that Atticus would not be taking the case, Atticus says, "Of course we'll take it" (148). Jean Louise is momentarily joyous that her father is the same defender of black people she saw him to be in her childhood and that the horrible White Citizens' Council speech was just an uncharacteristic moment. But immediately Atticus makes clear that he is not doing this because of his love for and debt to Zeebo's mother, Calpurnia, not to be sure that justice is done, but because he doesn't want the NAACP sending black lawyers into the community. "The NAACP-paid lawyers are standing around like buzzards down here waiting for things like this to happen—" (149). He makes clear that his objection is to their black lawyers, and he objects on every civil rights issue that would bring black people justice in the courtroom: "they [the NAACP] demand Negroes on the juries in such cases. . . . They subpoena the jury commissioners, they ask the judge to step down, they raise every trick in their books" (149). These are all reforms that may have saved Tom Robinson's life in *To Kill a Mockingbird.*

The tragedy in *Go Set a Watchman* is that Jean Louise, in a real sense, loses both her father and her mother during her trip home. Perhaps the most heartbreaking scene is her visit to Calpurnia, now a very old woman who had left her post in the Finch family after Jem's death. Frank, the young black man in jail, was Calpurnia's favorite grandson. He had much promise in being wait-listed for Tuskegee Institute, a traditional black college in Alabama. In Calpurnia's response to her, Jean Louise sees more evidence that relationships between the races have become more toxic. Calpurnia is cold to Jean Louise, is unmoved by Jean Louise's offer of help, and finally asks, "what are you all doing to us?" In short, what are you white people doing to us black people? Jean Louise is crushed, and looking into Calpurnia's face, she knows their relationship is hopeless: "in Calpurnia's eyes was no hint of compassion" (160). Jean Louise is compelled to ask Calpurnia if she hated them when they were her children. After a long pause, the answer seems to be no. Out in the car, Jean Louise tries unsuccessfully to comfort herself: "She loved us, I swear she loved us. She sat there in front of me and she didn't see me, she saw white folks" (161).

As she had in *To Kill a Mockingbird* when Scout was a child, Aunt Alexandra scolds her thoroughly when she finds that Jean Louise has visited Calpurnia: "nobody goes to see Negroes any more, not after what they've been doing to us. Besides being shiftless now they look at you sometimes with open insolence" (166). She goes on to say, often using racial slurs, that the NAACP has filled them with poison, that white people have always been so good to black people, but that now "that veneer of civilization's so thin that a bunch of uppity Yankee Negroes can shatter a hundred years' progress in five" (166). She also suggests that black people "carry cards," meaning that they are Communists.

Racism, Jean Louise suspects at the end of this long speech, has destroyed her and her personal relationships. Every white person she cherishes has told her that the awful changes she sees in race relations are "all on account of the Negroes . . . but it's no more the Negroes than I can fly and God knows, I might fly out the window any time now" (168).

Racism at the Coffee Party

It is scarcely a surprise to Jean Louise to meet with racism at the coffee party for upper-class young women that Aunt Alexandra gives for her. Her conversation with one, Hester, begins with reference to Frank's arrest and Hester's glee that they may have a good trial to amuse them. Jean Louise hears Aunt Alexandra commenting that Zeebo is uncivilized. He's still "in the trees," and it is sad what is happening to Calpurnia's family "but that's just the way they are and they can't help it" (173). Alexandra and the other guests complain about peaceful protests, marches in Montgomery, and black people trying to rise above their stations through attendance at the University of Alabama. Hester shows the fear in racism as she quotes from her husband, who believes there will be another Nat Turner uprising, that whites are "sitting on a keg of dynamite" (173). When Jean Louise brings up the black churches, Hester says it is all hypocrisy, that black leaders are like Mahatma Gandhi—Communists. It is common knowledge, says Hester, that the NAACP plans the overthrow of the South. In further criticism of black people, Hester says black people want to mongrelize the white race. Jean Louise answers that it takes two people, including a white one, to mongrelize the race. Whereupon Hester says she wasn't talking about upper-class women marrying black men, but "the trashy people" (177). Jean Louise reminds her that it used to be "gentlemen plantation owners who coupled with black women."

Jean Louise thinks of what she'd like to say to this woman, that she had never heard the racist slur uttered by a member of her family until now, that she had grown up with black people surrounding her, that poor as they were, she had never been given the idea that she was to hate or fear or mistreat one, that she was never taught to take advantage of a less fortunate person. "That is the way I was raised by a black woman and a white man" (179).

Another woman at the coffee party, Claudine, tells her what she considers to be an appalling story of finding a black woman eating right next to her in a diner in New York City. Jean Louise asks her why she was upset; did the woman hurt her in any way? No, Claudine answers, but Claudine got up and left immediately anyway. Claudine tells Jean Louise she must be blind not to even notice when a black man sits beside her on the bus.

Hester praises the fraternity boys whose demonstrations caused the trustees to purge the Alabama campus of Autherine Lucy. Jean Louise tries to correct her with reference to photographic evidence that most of those who marched in the streets were tire factory workers. In any case, the coffee party makes her more confused, more of an outsider on this issue of race.

Racism and Relationships: Revelations in Conversations about Race

Uncle Jack

When she approaches her Uncle Jack for clarity and assurance, he speaks to her in literary conundrums, suggesting that the causes of current racial problems are the 19th-century Industrial Revolution and the Civil War and Reconstruction, which continues to have an impact. "Up popped Tobacco Road [inhabited by the poorest whites], and up popped the ugliest, most shameful aspect of it all—the breed of white man who lived in open economic competition with freed Negroes" (196). In short, he seems to blame everything on the rise of the lower classes.

She replies that race relations are worse than she has ever seen them.

Hank's Rationalization

Her next confrontation is with Hank. Because of the racial bias she has observed in Hank, any romantic relationship with him is now impossible. But first she tries to understand his and Atticus's biased convictions that she has witnessed at the Maycomb Citizens' Council meeting. He brings up the Klan, which he wrong-headedly believes was once respectable and was just a political force, despite its documented violent history. In the course of their conversation, he astounds her with the information that forty years earlier, Atticus had actually joined the KKK for a time, his motive being to find out what made them tick. One thing Atticus found out was that the Wizard, or leader, of the group of lynchers and terrorists was the Methodist minister.

Atticus and Racism

The most traumatic and extensively treated confrontation over race is, of course, with her father, Atticus, her idol, who had once taught her "equality for all; special privileges for none."

Atticus is prepared for the conversation because, as she learns later, Uncle Jack has given him a heads up with a telephone call immediately after Jean Louise left his house. She begins with a specific: his deep involvement with the Maycomb Citizens' Council. He defends himself by responding that she has been reading newspapers that know nothing about the local group. It isn't like similar groups in north Alabama and Tennessee, which, he acknowledges, are involved with "wild threats and bombings and such." When he reminds her that, as she could see for herself, the members of the local group was made up of every man in the county, she brings up a particularly crooked citizen she had seen.

He makes things no better by giving her the reasons why he himself is part of the group: his objections to the federal government and the NAACP, asking her what her reaction had been to the Supreme Court's decision in *Brown v. Board of Education*. Jean Louise was furious, she says, because it violated the 10th amendment to the Constitution that guarantees states' rights. She says that after thinking about it, she realized that what she was angry about was not what the decision did, but the way it was done, suggesting at this point that integration could somehow have been accomplished by Congress and state legislatures. Still, the Supreme Court had offered a beginning. She didn't approve of the way they did it, "but they had to do it . . . Atticus, the time has come when we've got to do right—" (241). By that she means give "Negroes" a chance, which they don't have now. In answer to her father, she quotes key lines that appeared in *To Kill a Mockingbird*: "Equal rights for all; special privileges for none"— the definition of democracy.

It is at this point that Atticus reveals his commitment to racial segregation, based on his belief that blacks are an inferior race. "Have you ever considered that you can't have a set of backward people living among people advanced in one kind of civilization and have a social Arcadia?" (242). He continues this argument with his stated conviction that if black people get the vote in some counties with majority black populations, they will occupy every county seat even though unfit to govern.

Jean Louise, when challenged by Atticus, admits that she is something of a political conservative, but still argues vociferously against discrimination. The subject of the wall now comes up in conversation as she asks him why he had not explained when she was a child that "there was a fence around everything marked 'White Only'?" (243).

She then turns to a defense of the NAACP:

> "Atticus, the NAACP hasn't done half of what I've seen in the past two days. It's us."
>
> "Us?"
>
> "Yes sir, us. You. Has anybody in all the wrangling and high words over states' rights and what kind of government we should have, thought about helping the Negroes?"

She then lays out her views for Atticus: that the South and Congress should have worked to improve the lives of black people long ago, that the Supreme Court and the NAACP's hands were forced and that now the South was running from and denying the truth. "I think we deserve everything we've gotten from the NAACP and more" (245). At one point Atticus asks her if she is a Communist.

As she continues to embellish her argument, the idea of the fence comes up again: "Why," she asks Atticus, "did you imbue me with the idea of justice? Why didn't you make me a bigot like the rest of Maycomb when I was a child?—tell me: That Jesus loved all mankind, but there are different kind of men with separate fences around 'em, that Jesus meant that any man can go as far as he wants within that fence—" (249).

She tries to explain to Atticus that he has always been decent and caring and polite to black people, but that in regarding them as a race, he doesn't see them as human beings—he denies them hope. He is, she says, no better than Hitler; he just kills black people's souls instead of their bodies. As she leaves his office, she calls him a son-of-a-bitch.

Jean Louise's Southern People Are Not of Her Kind

After she goes back to the house from Atticus's office, she decides that this conversation about race impels her to cut short her vacation to Maycomb. Uncle Jack tries to explain how he sees the situation. He insists that both she and Atticus should tolerate one another on this matter of differing views of race, assuring her that Atticus would never condone the violence of the Klan, and that she has never thought in terms of race, herself. "You see only people" (270). More than once she or Jack considers her colorblind.

Uncle Jack rationalizes Atticus's racism by telling her that every person has his or her own watchman or conscience and she has developed her own, independent of Atticus's: "We wondered, sometimes, when your conscience and his would part company" (265).

At the end, despite the racism that Atticus has expressed, he tells her that he is proud of her "holding her ground for what she thinks is right— stand up to me first of all" (277).

So it is on the issue of race that she declares her own independent adulthood.

Further Reading

Clark, Culpepper. *The Schoolhouse Door: Segregation's Last Stand at the University of Alabama.* Oxford: Oxford University Press, 1993.

Kellogg, Charles Flint. *NAACP: A History of the National Association for the Advancement of Colored People.* Baltimore: Johns Hopkins University Press, 1967.

Kluger, Richard. *Simple Justice: The History of Brown v. Board of Education and Black America's Struggle for Equality.* New York: Alfred A. Knopf, 1976.

Lee, Harper. *Go Set a Watchman.* New York: HarperCollins, 2015.

Lee, Harper. *To Kill a Mockingbird.* Philadelphia: J. B. Lippincott, 1960. Warner Books paperback edition, 1982.

McMillen, Neil R. *The Citizens' Council: Organized Resistance to the Second Reconstruction, 1954–64.* Urbana: University of Illinois Press, 1994.

Tyson, Timothy. *The Blood of Emmett Till.* New York: Simon and Schuster, 2017.

Wade, Wyn Craig. *The Fiery Cross: The Ku Klux Klan in America.* New York: Oxford University Press, 1998.

Williamson, Joel. *A Rage for Order: Black/White Relations in the American South since Emancipation.* Oxford: Oxford University Press, 1986.

CHAPTER FIVE

Women's Issues and Gender

To Kill a Mockingbird and *Go Set a Watchman* are both stories of repressive walls—those between individuals, those set up by cultures—that stifle nature and happiness and potential, and even life itself. In Harper Lee's novels, the wall of race is represented by the prison fence that Tom Robinson scrambles over before he is shot. In *To Kill a Mockingbird*, the wall of stifling gender expectations is represented in Scout's mind by a "pink penitentiary." Gender and race are the dual major topics in *Go Set a Watchman*.

In the 1950s, at the time of the composition of the two novels, which is also the setting of *Go Set a Watchman*, women's issues had not come to the forefront, despite the 1949 appearance of Simone de Beauvoir's *The Second Sex*, which attacked the idea of the inferiority of women to men. Many women had worked outside the home during World War II (epitomized by "Rosie the Riveter"). But after the war, they were expected to go back to the home and take on subservient and limited roles as their husbands' mates and servants while the men assumed the jobs that women were paid to do during the war. Women were reminded that their places were properly in the domestic sphere. Even women who worked still carried the whole burden of housework and childcare.

Young Scout is in despair as she takes measure of the values and interests of the world of ladies she observes at the missionary society gathering, a world she is doomed to enter. These are the Southern ladies' values Scout realizes she despises: "I wondered at the world of women. . . . I must soon enter this world, where on its surface fragrant ladies rocked slowly, fanned gently, and drank cool water. But I was more at home in my father's world" (233).

Men, she believes, are kinder than these ladies. Men didn't make fun of you because of your clothing and, in her case, because she observed a trial in court. Despite their faults, men were more likeable: "Mr. Heck Tate did not trap you with innocent questions to make fun of you; even Jem was not highly critical unless you said something stupid. Ladies seemed to live in faint horror of men, seemed unwilling to approve wholeheart-edly of them. . . . there was something about them [men] that I instinc-tively liked" (234).

One reason for liking men more than women popped into her mind from the general conversation—men weren't hypocrites, at least to the extent that she sees hypocrisy in the missionary society ladies. While Atticus and Calpurnia are driving out to give the heartbreaking news of Tom's death to his wife, the ladies carry on: "And so they went, down the row of laughing women, around the dining room, refilling coffee cups dishing out goodies as though their only regret was the temporary domes-tic disaster of losing Calpurnia" (237).

Expectations of Women and Family Life

Scout's and Jean Louise's experience of nontraditional families shaped their unconventional views of girlhood and womanhood. Both novels were composed in the 1950s when the image of the ideal American family was at its peak in movies and on television. *Father Knows Best, The Adven-tures of Ozzie and Harriet, Leave It to Beaver,* and even *I Love Lucy* were typical. The ideal family consisted of the professional working father, the stay-at-home, cookie-making mother, and two or three well-behaved chil-dren. They experienced no social or psychological conflict or trauma. Of all the households mentioned in *To Kill a Mockingbird,* only two come close to this ideal: Tom Robinson's and Dolphus Raymond's. Yet neither really fit the American ideal because Tom's family is black and Dolphus's family is "mixed race." It isn't even clear that Dolphus and the black mother of his children are married. The rumor is that his white bride shot herself on her wedding day when she found out that Dolphus had a black lover. His children, being "mixed" children, don't belong anywhere. Jem explains the situation to Scout: "Colored folks won't have 'em because they're half white; white folks won't have 'em 'cause they're colored, so they're just in-between, don't belong anywhere." Some of the children don't even live with the family because Dolphus has shipped them up North where they are better tolerated.

Nor are the Radleys illustrative of the all-American, ideal family even though they at one time consisted of father, mother, and two boys. But even back when the senior Mr. Radley was alive, it was an isolated, poisonous household that had nothing to do with its neighbors: "The misery of that house began many years before Jem and I were born. . . . The shutters and doors of the Radley house were closed on Sundays. . . . [T]o climb the Radley front steps and call, 'He-y,' of a Sunday afternoon was something their neighbors never did" (9).

Scout and Jem have no living biological mother and they call their father by his first name, Atticus, not Daddy. And Atticus treats them like adults.

The Ewell household has no mother and is tainted with incest and cruelty, filth and drunkenness.

Aunt Alexandra, when she moves in with Atticus, leaves her family behind at Finch's Landing. When Scout and Jem realize that Aunt Alexandra is moving into their house, Scout blurts out what she immediately realizes is a rude question, in essence, "Won't you miss your husband?" She knows that he doesn't matter to his wife—present or absent makes little difference.

Dill's father has deserted the family, and his mother, who is never present in the novel, sends him around to live with various relatives. As Dill explains to Scout, he feels, even when he is with his mother and stepfather, that he is emotionally deserted: "Dill's voice went on steadily in the darkness: 'The thing is, what I'm tryin' to say is—they *do* get on a lot better without me, I can't help them any. They ain't mean'" (143).

The neighbors are all unmarried and childless. Even the widows are referred to as "Miss": Miss Maudie, Mrs. Dubose, Miss Rachel Haverford, Miss Stephanie Crawford. There is one bachelor, Mr. Avery. Uncle Jack Finch never marries. The three women teachers mentioned in the novel are single, as was required in the 1930s and usually the 1940s.

Discrimination in Education and Vocation

To appreciate how far Scout deviated from the accepted role of little girls, the reader has to have a grasp of the everyday life of women and girls at the time of the setting of the novel. The discriminatory treatment of women at the time is an old story that continues even in the 21st century—seen in newspaper reports about the gaps between men's and women's salaries at all levels. At the time of *To Kill a Mockingbird*, women had only had the vote for 12 years and the text makes clear that women in Alabama could not serve on juries and had no part in governance. The only women in the novel who work outside their own domestic spheres are Tom Robinson's wife, Calpurnia, and Scout's teachers.

White women were expected to be wives and mothers, period. Their venue was the house. If they were poor and therefore compelled to work, their grueling jobs were on farms or in factories. With some training, they could be secretaries and clerks, beauticians and nurses. But, in the last case, prejudice against female nurses still persisted. (Even as late as the first decades of the 20th century, nurses, like actresses, were considered little better than prostitutes because they had to touch men's bodies.)

The only profession open to educated women was teaching and then only as long as they remained unmarried. Teachers were forbidden to marry for the length of their contracts. Much to the detriment of school-children, they were often taught by women who had no inclination or talent for dealing with children, because that's all they were allowed to do.

The women in the missionary society make fun of Scout by asking her if she plans to be a lawyer. The jibe is meant to humiliate her because very few women in the 1930s could look forward to professional school, even though Harper Lee's older sister became a practicing lawyer and Lee, her-self, was able to attend law school sporadically.

The general prejudice in systems of higher education dictated that women not be allowed to attend colleges and universities with men. Most states had special colleges for women: for instance, Winthrop College in South Carolina, Livingston Normal School in Alabama, and the Women's College of North Carolina in Greensboro. This was also true of the major-ity of private universities, Radcliffe College of Harvard University being particularly noteworthy. Not until 1920 were women admitted to any portion of Harvard University and then only to the Graduate School of Education. Not until 1963 could women apply to all departments of the University of North Carolina–Chapel Hill as freshmen and sophomores and even then special rules—primarily regarding curfews—applied to women that did not apply to men. The situation in Alabama was vastly different in that, through the efforts of Julia Tutwiler, women were admit-ted in the late 19th century to the University of Alabama, Harper Lee's alma mater, and its law school.

This discrimination girls and women lived with is unabashedly articu-lated in the novel by the clergy. Miss Maudie tells Scout that the "foot-washing Baptists" who yell at her for her pride in growing beautiful flowers think women are sinful "by definition" (45). The "impurity" of women is something Scout has heard from the pulpit of her own church, and she is reminded of that when they attend Cal's church. The minister preaches about sin: women, he tells the congregation, are the worst trou-blemakers. The favorite topic of both white and black clergy is the dangerousness and moral weakness of women. Scout concludes that they are obsessed with the idea of women as temptresses. She asks Miss Maudie if this is why Boo Radley is isolated in his house, to protect him from women. From school to social life to the church, women are everywhere hemmed in by expectations of "ladylike" behavior.

Language

Partly to avoid the stigma of the temptress, it was expected of little girls to be soft-spoken, demure, and refined in their speech. Older ladies at the time even gave private lessons in elocution to girls, to teach them to speak in a genteel manner. No proper little girl would dream of using coarse, loud language, bad grammar, or curse words. Scout consistently does all three. She tells Miss Maudie, "Atticus don't ever do anything to Jem and me in the house that he don't do in the yard" (46). "Ain't" is a standard word in her vocabulary.

When Uncle Jack comes from Nashville for Christmas, he learns to his horror that Scout has begun using curse words. When he jokes with her, she replies, "Aw, that's a damn story" (78). Atticus tells his brother that Scout has been "cussing" all the time recently, and Scout thinks to herself that it may be an effective strategy: if Atticus found out that she was cussing at school, maybe he wouldn't make her go. Despite Atticus's advice to his brother to just stop paying attention to the cursing, Jack decides to have a talk with her and asks, "You like words like damn and hell now, don't you?" Her cousin Francis reports later that she has called him a "whore lady," though she confesses to Uncle Jack that she doesn't know what "whore lady" means. But when Uncle Jack, upon hearing her cursing, asks her if she doesn't want to grow up to be a lady, she answers, "not particularly" (79).

Scout and Expectations of Girls

Atticus runs a gender-neutral household and defends Scout's unladylike attire and language. That there is a distinction between expectations of males and females is impressed upon her not by Atticus but by her brother Jem's derisive remarks about girlishness. When she refuses to retrieve the tire Jem and Dill have been rolling her in (after it crashes into the Radley house), Jem says, "I swear, Scout, sometimes you act so much like a girl it's mortifyin'" (38). When she objects to yet another risky attempt to reach Boo Radley, she reports that he told her that "I was being a girl, that girls always imagined things, that's why other people hated them so, and if I started behaving like one I could just go off and find some to play with" (41). This, of course, emphasizes her having no little girl friends. When Jem is 12, he changes his approach and scolds her for *not* being like a girl and "not acting right" (115).

The young Scout's life is nothing like that of the typical little girl of her time, something she mentions repeatedly. For instance, though some schools offered or even required girls to take physical education, they were never encouraged to be athletic. They usually played in the house with other little girls. Their playthings were dolls, often baby dolls, doll clothing, little china tea sets, and stuffed animals. Scout adds "little stoves" and "add-a-pearl necklaces" to that list of what typical girls were interested in. Little girls liked to dress up in fancy clothes and have tea parties. They learned to dance demurely in their white gloves and long dresses and to arrange flowers at the junior garden club.

Instead of getting a doll for Christmas, Scout and Jem ask for and get rifles. Instead of having tea parties, she and Dill play football. Instead of playing house, she makes herself a fort out of tires, crates, and other rubbish from which she can aim her rifle. In unladylike fashion, she has physical fights with boys, trying with some success at school to beat up Cecil Jacobs and Walter Cunningham; to beat up her cousin Francis at Finch's Landing; and later, at home, her brother Jem. She rubs Walter's "nose in the dirt" (22) and "split my knuckle to the bone on his [Francis's] front teeth" (84). Although Jem is much older than she, "I threw myself at him as hard as I could, hitting, pulling, pinching, gouging. What had begun as a fist-fight became a brawl" (138).

Scout's associates could not be more atypical of the little girls of her age. She plays with two boys—her brother, Jem, and Dill. Her other associates are adults, like Atticus and the eccentric Miss Maudie. Not one other young girl her age has a role or reference in her story. The only classmates she mentions are boys: Little Chuck Little, Walter Cunningham, Burris Ewell, and Cecil Jacobs. The only young visitor to her house is Walter, who comes once to lunch. The only people she visits are adults: Miss Maudie who also wears overalls and hates her house and Mrs. Dubose, under duress.

The Key Matter of Attire

Gender in both novels turns on the matter of attire expected of ladies and little girls who aspired to be ladies. And, lest girls were not inclined to follow custom, there were institutional rules to force their compliance with accepted cultural codes. Little girls wore dresses and skirts—period.

Old school handbooks and unpublished memories of life in the 1940s, even up through the 1960s, are sources for what "nice" girls were expected to wear. Hair was either parted in the middle or in ringlets or braids, none of which Scout does.

One good source of girls' fashion comes from the 1935 Sears catalog. All the clothing offered for little girls were dresses except for one snowsuit that included pants. All the dresses had full skirts to just above the knee (Shirley Temple style) with puffy sleeves and white socks and shoes in summer weather. Most illustrations show little girls wearing hats. Women's dresses at the time all went to well below the knee.

Other memories are provided by Millicent Harrelson and Sylvia Zupp, who attended a small women's college, called Limestone, in South Carolina, in the 1950s. A young woman could not leave the dormitory where she lived in long pants or jeans, unless she had permission to go on a picnic. If she had to take a telephone call in the dorm lobby and was not properly attired in a dress or skirt, she had to wear a raincoat to cover herself up. No tennis shoes were allowed except in the sports venue (Harrelson and Zupp interviews).

Meg Foster has collected information about required dress rules for women from a number of college handbooks in the 1950s ("Absurd Rules"). At Spelman College for women in Atlanta, students had to wear stockings instead of socks and their hair had to be styled. Rules existed governing the wearing of jewelry and makeup. At most colleges, Limestone and Ohio University included, women were required to wear hats and gloves to church and Sunday dinner. At the University of Missouri, women could not wear scarves or slacks in dorm lounges or dining rooms. Grown women, like Aunt Alexandra, wore girdles. In *To Kill a Mockingbird*, Miss Stephanie Crawford is in the typical out-of-house attire of hat and gloves when she leaves to observe a courthouse trial for rape.

Compare all this with Scout, a little girl whose customary attire, whether she is running around the neighborhood or going to town, even the courthouse, is overalls, and says, "I was usually mud-splashed and covered with sand" (132). Mrs. Dubose, who insults Atticus and the children, makes no bones about her disapproval, shouting from the porch, "What are you doing in those overalls? You should be in a dress and camisole, young lady!" (101). In *Go Set a Watchman*, we learn from a flashback that in the summer, Scout had worn nothing *under* her overalls.

But it is Aunt Alexandra who brings the subject of Scout's boyish appearance to the forefront—Aunt Alexandra who is like Mount Everest: "throughout my life she was cold and there" (77). Scout concludes that Alexandra's constant nagging of Atticus "has something to do with my going around in overalls" (81). She was "fanatical" on the subject. Aunt Alexandra even explains her motives in coming to help him with the children partly in terms of Scout's unfeminine behavior, including her attire: "'Jem's growing up now and you are too,' she said to me. 'We decided that it would be best for you to have some feminine influence. It won't be many years, Jean Louise, before you become interested in clothes and boys'" (127). Scout's answer to Aunt Alexandra remains unspoken. "Cal's a girl, it would be many years before I would be interested in boys, I would never be interested in clothes" (127).

Scout's overalls are a matter of amusement and derision among the ladies of the missionary society, who know full well that she doesn't dress like a proper little girl. For the social hour, Scout wears her pink Sunday dress, a petticoat, and proper shoes, because she is expected to appear at the meeting. She worries that if she spills anything on the dress, Calpurnia will have to wash it (Claire Fortune describes the arduous process in a letter to me) because the next day is Sunday. When Scout enters the living room, Miss Maudie asks her where her "britches" are, and she answers, "Under my dress." The whole room of pastels and perfume, except for Miss Maudie, explodes in laughter (229).

Some of the "old school Southern rules" cited by Jenny Bradley are scarcely what Scout would follow: wear hats and gloves; if you don't know someone's name, call them "honey" or "darlin'"; always call your father Daddy; never swear in public; young people stand up when an older person enters the room ("Ten Old School Southern Rules"). The only one Atticus would enforce is the last.

It must also be considered that the missionary society meeting occurs soon after Tom Robinson's trial, and the whole town is aware that the three children attended, somewhat hidden in the balcony. When Miss Stephanie Crawford taunts Scout with the question of what she wants to be when she grows up, she thinks to herself about several professions, including aviator. It is important to note that women at the time were rarely accepted into law schools or the legal profession, so when Miss Stephanie, meanly referring to Scout's unacceptable presence in court, says, "Why shoot, I thought you wanted to be a lawyer, you've already commenced going to court," the assembled ladies begin laughing at her again (230). Scout responds that she wants to grow up to be a lady, whereupon the overalls subject pops up again. Miss Stephanie tells her that she won't be able to do that until she starts wearing dresses more often.

The members of this group, except for Miss Maudie, are definitely not her models, no matter what she grows up to be, but she does study Calpurnia, hoping she can find out some of the skills expected of a true, proper girl.

Stereotyping the "Tomboy"

In addition to Scout's disgust and difficulties with traditional Southern young ladyhood, several other incidents in *To Kill a Mockingbird* have led some readers to conclude that Scout does not fundamentally identify as female. First, Dill is based on Truman Capote, an openly gay man in adulthood. Second is the "morphodite" snowman the kids make, who is a mixture of Mr. Avery and Miss Maudie. Another is Scout's observation that because Jem has gotten moodier after Tom's death, he has become more like a girl.

But a more plausible explanation is that Scout resists the traditionally imposed values and restraints placed on girls and women, rather than womanhood or heterosexuality itself. When Scout revisits Maycomb in adulthood, in *Go Set a Watchman*, written about the same time, she is physically, romantically attracted to her boyfriend, Hank.

This point of view that girls can be tomboys without expressing dissatisfaction with their gender is well articulated by Lisa Selin Davis in an op-ed column in the *New York Times*. She writes about her daughter who wears pants and most of whose friends are boys. Davis urges her readers to recognize that girls who don't conform to the roles and models of girls are still girls and should be respected and recognized even when they do not follow the "narrow confines of gender roles." At the same time that "we have broadened our awareness of and support for gender nonconformity, we've narrowed what we think a boy or a girl can look like or do" (A25).

The following full quote from *To Kill a Mockingbird* about the walls of gender, particularly the stifling code inflicted on the Southern belle, is one of the most powerful images in a book of strong prose. It is triggered by the arrival on the scene of Aunt Alexandra: "My heart sank: me. I felt the starched walls of a pink cotton penitentiary closing in on me, and for the second time in my life I thought of running away. Immediately" (136).

Gender in *Go Set a Watchman*

Marriage and Maycomb

Go Set a Watchman is Jean Louse's unhappy confrontation with what it means to be a woman in Maycomb, Alabama, and what marriage means anywhere. In a conversation about her failure to commit to marriage with Henry, she gives her impression of the typical New York marriage, though "the application is universal" (48): the wives get bored and start complaining; the men find mistresses, eventually go back to their wives who start complaining again; and it starts all over. She sees the same thing happening with the Birmingham social set: the wife would typically be in misery because she would realize she had married the wrong man. "The hollering and the high-mindedness over, all that would be left would be another shabby little affair a la the Birmingham country club set" (15).

She struggles increasingly in the novel with the idea that there is no way she can take on the life of a woman in Maycomb. In matters womanly, she is not their kind and cannot live among them. Intellectually and sexually, she loves men, but she has no use for women and the lives women live in Maycomb.

The Tomboy in Memory

The tomboy Scout of old is often on Jean Louise's mind. She wonders if Maycomb after all these years remembers "the juvenile desperado, hell-raiser extraordinaire" that she was back when she was a girl. She remembers that she had never thought of herself as a girl when she was a child. She had occupied herself with "reckless, pummeling activity; fighting, football, climbing," keeping up with her older brother, and eager for any win at physical contests. She had been "a howling tom boy" (116, 117). A recollection of childhood enters her head of being forbidden from visiting another little girl friend because the friend's mother regarded her as being "too rough" (13). Moreover, she recalls being terrified to be compelled to have to "go into a world of femininity, a world she despises, could not comprehend nor defend herself against, a world that did not want her" (116).

Jean Louise attests to having grown beyond the most extreme of her tomboy behavior: "she had turned from an overalled, fractious, gun-slinging creature into a reasonable facsimile of a human being" (13). When Atticus says in their conversation that he sees two people in her, she asks if one is a tomboy and one a woman. And after her rude remarks to Aunt Alexandra, she apologizes, saying, "I'm not much of a lady, Aunty." And she confesses that she still moves like a 13-year-old boy, and "abjured most feminine adornments" (13).

Certainly the Jean Louise of *Go Set a Watchman* is portrayed as a grown-up tomboy for many reasons: her attire, her language, her associates, her interests, and her general dismissal of the suffocating and frivolous role of the Southern lady.

Jean Louise and Expected Appearance

Culturally approved appearance—dresses, hats, lipstick—represent all she despises about the town in which she grew up. She ridicules the guests at the coffee party: "The magpies arrived at 10:30, on schedule. . . . They wore gloves and hats, and smelled to high heaven of attars, perfumes, eaus, and bath powder. Their makeup would have put an Egyptian draftsman to shame, and their clothes—particularly their shoes—had definitely been purchased in Montgomery or Mobile: Jean Louise spotted A. Nachman, Gayfers, Levy's, Hammel's on all sides of the living room" (168). One of Jean Louise's least favorite memories is being "stuffed" as a child by Calpurnia into a stiff pink dress and patent leather shoes.

By contrast, Jean Louise's ungenteel attire is the first matter to come up in the novel. In the fifth paragraph, she explains changing into what she calls her "Maycomb clothes." These are not the clothes characteristic of women who live in Maycomb, but what she feels comfortable in on vacation: "grey slacks, a black sleeveless blouse, white socks and loafers" (4). As she dons her slacks, she can hear her aunt's disapproval from four hours away.

Jean Louise's slacks are who she is and parallel her complicated relationship to her family and Maycomb. Southern appearances continue to be at the forefront of the novel—a recurrent theme running through it—in the brief but repeated admonitions of Aunt Alexandra. Soon after she arrives at her father's home the quarrel erupts: Her aunt sniffed, "I do wish this time you'd try to dress better while you're home. Folks in town get the wrong impression of you. They think you are—ah—slumming" (21). Jean Louise characterizes this first remark as another struggle in a Hundred Years' War that has gone on for her whole life—26 years.

As she and Hank prepare to go out on a date, and she asks him if she can wear her slacks, he answers "no," obviously to appease Aunt Alexandra who thanks him for it. On Sunday, when Jean Louise heads for the courthouse after church, obviously having changed into her slacks, Aunt Alexandra calls to her, "You aren't going to town "Like That" (104). And when Jean Louise returns so traumatized by the White Citizens' Council Meeting that she is physically sick and vomiting, Aunt Alexandra's only concern is that she has visited out of the family Like That, repeating it when she finds that Jean Louise has gone to the men's meeting Like That. Again and again throughout the novel she tells Jean Louise to go change her clothes.

Anticipating her aunt's wishes, when she drives Atticus to work, she puts on a dress, but Aunt Alexandra is not satisfied and instructs her to put on lipstick as well.

Unladylike Language

Jean Louise's language, as well as her aversion to dresses, continues to brand her as unladylike. After Aunt Alexandra infuriates her with a lecture on why she shouldn't marry Hank because of his social rank and family history, Jean Louise tells her "Aunty, . . . why don't you go pee in your shoe" (938). When she and Hank are joking with one another, she says, "Go to hell, then." She yells out "*Damn*ation!" when she hits her head on the door of Hank's car. And when she returns from her talk with Atticus, she appalls Aunt Alexandra with her "Yankee" expression: "for Christ's sake" (257). But the *pièce de résistance* comes at the climax of her defiance of her father when she twice calls him "a son of a bitch," one time enhancing the label: a "ring-tailed old son of a bitch." This language is referred to three more times, when Atticus reports it to his brother Jack, when Jack brings it up with Jean Louise, and when she and Atticus refer to it when they reach a truce. Atticus has apparently never come across the ring-tailed expression and Jean Louise claims to have learned it in Maycomb.

Jean Louise's Memories and the Proper Southern Lady

In other ways, she and everyone else knows that she is still not a proper Southern lady. For example, she has no female friends. The girlfriends she did have in high school were from the despised Old Sarum rank. She was never friends with and has no idea what to say to the young ladies of the coffee party, only three of whom are unmarried like herself. She still hangs out with men (Atticus, Hank, and Uncle Jack).

What occupies her leisure is not a series of ladies' parties but a man's game—golf. Some women played golf on public courses and a few were very good at it, but the numbers of women golfers were not many in the 1950s, because women were not admitted as full members into private golf clubs. The old saying was that "golf" stood for "Gentlemen Only, Ladies Forbidden," that women talk too much and play too slowly and not well. But it is her father's game, despised by Aunt Alexandra because Jean Louise, Jem, and Atticus have ruined the carpet, by practicing their putting in the living room. Jean Louise immediately finds a putter and a spittoon full of golf balls by the hearth. And she makes a date to play golf with her father.

In very unladylike fashion, she sneaks into an all-men's meeting in the courthouse and jumps in the water at night at Finch's Landing with her clothes on.

Three of the extensive memory sequences of the past that Jean Louise summons up have to do with her encroaching womanhood. None of them are pleasant. The first is the onset of her menstrual period; the second is the fear that a boy's kiss has made her pregnant; and the third is the disaster that ensues when she decides to wear "false bosoms" to the prom.

In the first, of sixth grade, which began as a wonderful year learning from the Old Sarum boys how to shoot craps, chew tobacco, play volleyball, and tumble in the dust playing a tag game by the name of Hot-Grease-in-the-Kitchen, her world fell apart. When her menstrual period began, she was physically handicapped—"encumbered by accoutrements" she was unused to, finding it difficult to walk, much less take part in rough games the boys invited her to play with them. This inability led her to the Old Sarum girls, who introduce her to their views of womanhood and women.

> "You've got the Curse."
> "The what?"
> "The Curse. Curse o' Eve. If Eve hadn't et the apple we wouldn't have it. You feel bad?" (127)

The second memory of growing into womanhood came as a result of her complete ignorance of the birds and the bees. A boy she had helped pass a test, Albert Coningham, French-kissed her at school as a thank-you. Not long after, the Old Sarum girls see her complete lack of knowledge about where babies come from and, in trying to educate her, give her the wrong idea when they tell her it all begins with French-kissing. She becomes convinced that she is pregnant. For nine months she is in such agony about this that she plans to kill herself the day before she thinks the baby is coming. It is only when her attempt to jump into the water tower is foiled by Hank that she confesses her fears to Calpurnia. Calpurnia takes it upon herself to give the motherless child a lesson in sex education, and, subsequently, relief from what Jean Louise dreaded as another curse of womanhood.

The third memory is of the prom when she tries on her dress and becomes unhappy with her "bowling pin" figure—"which was the way all girls more or less were" when they were 14. To correct this, she buys falsies to give her figure a more womanly look. She remembers the thrill of dancing with Henry and the admiration of her classmates. But a disaster happens when Henry rushes her outside to show her that she has had a clothing malfunction. Her false bosoms have moved to the side. She solves this problem of premature womanhood by flinging them into the bushes.

Romance and Sexuality

Even as Jean Louise despises the Southern belle culture that threatens to stifle her, in adolescence her preference for male playmates has become a physical attraction to boys. She is interested but not obsessed. She remembers Henry's two kisses on the night of the prom when her cheeks grew "hot," and she asked her father if Hank was too old for her. She adored him throughout her teens.

Something of a tomboy Jean Louise may still be when she returns to Maycomb in *Go Tell a Watchman*, but also romantically drawn to men as well. Every time she comes home she goes out with Henry ("Hank") Clinton. When he picks her up at the station on this visit, they kiss in public. She acts surprised, and he says he would even kiss her on the courthouse steps. She thinks that she can never get tired of watching him move, and "he found something so intensely feminine about her."

In response to the first of many marriage proposals on this trip, she replies that she won't marry him but she'll have an affair with him.

Their affection continues when he picks her up on a date. His "masculine" smell prompts her to suddenly throw "her arms around his waist" and nuzzle "her head on his chest" (39). As they leave the house, she thinks she is closer to accepting his marriage proposal than ever before. Their date that night at Finch's Landing is romantic, beginning with his second proposal and a kiss. How far their love-making goes is mysteriously unspecified: "She took his head in her arms. . . . Henry, kissing her drew her down to him on the floor of the landing" (78). It was some time later before she broke it up.

At church the next morning, with rumors swirling about a naked moonlight swim, Uncle Jack jokes, "Your guilty lover's waitin' within" (91), and Hank winks at her as he passes the collection plate.

Rejection of Marriage

Even if Jean Louise had not become disillusioned with Hank because of his political views, even though she had come close to loving him and had seen him as one of her kind, there is scarcely a possibility that she would have married him. She had resisted his proposals on previous visits as she does now. When she tells him just after she gets off the train that she'll have an affair with him, but won't marry him, she speculates that marrying him would be an easy way out for her, but realizes that she always chooses the hard way. What crosses her mind is what she sees as the stereotypical Alabama—actually Birmingham—country club marriage. It starts out with a house and children and ends in misery and "shabby," extramarital affairs, as the couple finds the person they should have married. Immediately upon her arrival, the only local story she hears is about the divorce, on ground of adultery, of the Merriweathers, once viewed as an ideal couple who had been married for 42 years. The independent-minded Jean Louise decides to keep being a spinster for now and apologizes to Henry (15).

When the topic of marriage again arises at dinner with Henry, she expresses some of the same reservations, this time with reference to what she observed about New York marriages—that the typical marriage cycle proceeds in misery and love affairs. She's afraid, she says, of marrying the wrong man, but the conversation is interrupted just after he asks her why he isn't the right man. Later, her description of the ideal husband prompts Henry to observe that it sounds like she's looking for a father instead of a husband.

She jokes that she might marry him if they can live at the Landing instead of in Maycomb. On the way home she considers that it might work, but she truthfully isn't the wifely type: she's not domestic, can't cook, can't talk to ladies and visit, won't wear hats, and would probably drop the babies and kill them (80).

After she has seen him at the White Citizens' Council and just before her traumatic talk with Atticus, she has coffee with Henry to lay to rest any possibility of their marrying. When she gets the impression from Hank that a woman's marriage means losing her own identity, she tells him that, if marriage results in that, she will never marry, not anyone, and especially not him. He has assumed that their differing social/political views would be transcended in marriage. She notes that in his list of desires for his life, marriage and family come last.

In Jean Louise's recollection of her sex education conversation, the marriage of her parents is painted as being very affectionate, but in all the years after her mother's death, Atticus has never remarried. In their confrontation, Jean Louise brings this up, revealing how she reads the Southern belle she can never be: "Why, in the name of God didn't you marry again? Marry some dim-witted Southern lady who would have raised me right? Turned me into a simpering mealy-mouthed magnolia type who bats her eyelashes and crosses her hands and lives for nothing but her lil' ole hus-band?" (249).

Jean Louise's visit brings up the stories of several failed or non-marriages and what she sees as the trivialization of women through marriage. No positive ones are mentioned. The first is Aunt Alexandra, hardly a sympathetic character, once married to a man who, in effect, dumped her, sending word by a servant that he was now living in his fishing cabin and wasn't planning to ever come home again. His decision had little effect on his wife and her lively social life. Nor can Alexandra summon up much enthusiasm for her devoted son who has settled in Birmingham. Her decades-long "courtship" with Cousin Edgar has never gone anywhere.

Jean Louise runs into Helen, Calpurnia's son Zeebo's wife, from whom he has been separated for many years. They are back together now (because Zeebo is old), but in the intervening years Zeebo has had about five failed marriages.

Many comments about marriages, seemingly happy, at the coffee party convince her that marriage is not for her and that she, especially, could never be a married Southern belle in Maycomb. Marriage, as she relates it to Hank, is a life of trivia to which she could not and would not subject herself: "They talk incessantly about the things they do, and I don't know how to do the things they do. If we married—if I married anybody from this town—these would be my friends, and I couldn't think of a thing to say to them. . . . I'd be churched to death, bridge-partied to death, called upon to give book reviews at the Amanuensis Club, expected to be part of the community" (173).

As the "magpies" pour into their living room, she divides them into four categories: the Newly Weds, the Diaper Set, the Light Brigade, and the Perennial Hopefuls—women with whom she was never even friendly when she lived in Maycomb.

The Newly Weds "chatter smugly" about their husbands' diets and weight. The Diaper Set speak of toilet training, sucking fingers, and "the cu-utest, absolutely the *cutest* sweatshirt you've ever seen: it's got a little red elephant and 'Crimson Tide' written right across the front" (169) (the Crimson Tide being Alabama's football team). The somewhat older Light Brigade, in their thirties, chatter about bridge, clubs, appliances, and gossip about other women. The three Perennial Hopefuls are the only unmarried women, looked down upon by the other women. They talk about the air conditioning at their work, food, and church, and themselves make fun of another woman.

The Independent Woman

Jean Louise continues to grow up on her visit to her father's home in Maycomb, Alabama. Her role as a daughter, her relationship to her father is challenged and changed. She loses the father she thought she had. And she loses her only mother—Calpurnia—who turns her away. But she remains an independent-minded young woman who could never be the kind of lady she sees in Maycomb, never share the values, interests, and politics she sees reflected in the aunt who tried to raise her, and her contemporaries at the party. Nor could she be the kind of wife Hank would require, nor anything but his friend, despite her physical attraction to him.

Further Reading

Baber, Kristine H., and Katherine R. Allen. *Women and Families: Feminist Reconstructions.* New York: Guilford Press, 1992.

Bradley, Jenny. "Ten Old School Southern Rules." *Odyssey on Line,* July 1, 2014.

Davis, Lisa Selin. "Girls Can Still Be Tomboys." *New York Times,* April 19, 2017, A25.

Falk, Gerhard. *End of the Patriarchy.* Lanham, MD: University Press of America, 2016.

Foster, Meg. "The Absurd Rules for College Women That Were Actually Enforced in the 1950s." http://historybuff.com/.

Friedan, Betty. *The Feminine Mystique.* New York: Dell, 1963.

Harvey, Brett. *The Fifties: A Woman's Oral History.* New York: HarperCollins, 1993.

Lee, Harper. *Go Set a Watchman.* New York: HarperCollins, 2015.

Lee, Harper. *To Kill a Mockingbird.* Philadelphia: J. B. Lippincott, 1960. Warner Books paperback edition, 1982.

Mair, Lewine. "Gentleman Only, Ladies Forbidden—a History." *Women's Golf Journal,* no. 2 (2017). https://womensgolfjournal.com/golf/no-women-allowed/.

Phillips, Anne. *Gender and Culture.* Cambridge: Polity Press, 2010.

Starrett, Helen E. *The Charm of Fine Manners.* Philadelphia: J. B. Lippincott, 1920.

"Women's Roles in the 1950s." In *American Decades,* edited by Judith S. Baughman et al., vol. 6: *1950–1959,* 278–80. Farmington Hills, MI: Gale Group, 2005.

Yates, Gayle Graham. *What Women Want: The Ideas of the Movement.* Cambridge, MA: Harvard University Press, 1975.

CHAPTER SIX

The Question of Social Class

Social class is a key issue in both of Harper Lee's novels, but it is treated in a more comprehensive and complicated way in *To Kill a Mockingbird*. Class or ranks in the 1930s had roots in the plantation system. At the top of the social ladder, before the Civil War, there were plantations owners, rich in land and slaves, who did little toil themselves, except sometimes managing their own investments in slaves or cotton. In the 1930s, social rank still had everything to do with just how much land a person owned. Beneath the large landowners in the antebellum South were small farmers, many of whom had several slaves. At the bottom of white society were dirt-poor, landless, tenant farmers. For the most part, members of no class had anything to do socially with members of any other class except their own. After Reconstruction, the ranks of large plantation owners, often called the Bourbons, dwindled, now largely being deprived of slave labor, but they continued to hold onto land and political power. By the 1930s, however, many had been replaced politically by populists of the middle and upper middle class who were still socially regarded as beneath the "old families." Even here, among village merchants, class divisions prevailed as larger shop owners with somewhat higher-end merchandise, for example, were regarded with more respect than owners of "mom and pop" small businesses. Below them were the same small farm owners, and then, tenant farmers. Separate from all these classes were black people.

Historical Background

Even with the promise of what many saw as a better life in urban factories, many poor farmers preferred to hold onto their land rather than move. Tenant farmers, like some of the Old Sarum residents, could expect to make only $10 a month. Clarence Cason gives a detailed picture of the dire exploitative financial circumstances of the rural poor, who work on farms owned by absentee landlords: "In March the typical tenant borrows about $200 from his landlord or banker. Of this sum, $50 may be designated for the fertilizer dealer, another $50 for the stock-feed merchant, and $10 for interest. In September or October, with luck, he may sell three bales of cotton for $200. . . . Then the farmer pays off his loan and has left about $15 for each of the six months until the next March" (32).

In the 1920s and 1930s, in some areas of the South, land ownership and literacy were still required of all poor whites as well as blacks in order to vote. Such laws effectively disenfranchised the poor. It is not clear whether this is true in Maycomb County, as Tom Robinson's jury is made up of lower-class whites, whose names were taken from voting rolls.

Cason, writing in 1935, paints a picture of lower-class life in the South at the time of *To Kill a Mockingbird.* Many poor whites began taking advantage of New Deal programs to ease their financial burdens, especially (as is mentioned in *To Kill a Mockingbird*), those under the National Recovery Administration. Still, diseases like hookworm and pellagra plagued the lower classes of the 1930s, "implying an unacceptable social status" (*90° in the Shade*, 13) Some of these diseases came from the children having to go barefoot, as Cason describes in a scene in South Carolina: "six or eight ragged children were eating green plums, their bare feet clutching the loose soil of a red clay embankment" (30).

As Wayne Flynt writes in *Alabama in the Twentieth Century*, and as we see in *To Kill a Mockingbird*, there were social divisions between poor people. They were either "poor but proud" or "po' white trash" (186). This distinction is not made in *Go Set a Watchman* where the hard-working Hank, with a law degree, is repeatedly referred to as "trash" even though his childhood background was respectable but poor. Flynt writes of distinctions in the black community as well where the lightness or darkness of one's skin, one's job, dress, and education determined one's social placement (186).

Both blacks and whites were exploited by large cotton growers in Alabama. Often black workers had the advantage of being hired over whites because they would accept lower pay and were more manageable than whites.

As textiles, steel factories, and mines came south (as in nearby Birmingham), plantation owners became mill owners and poor farm workers constituted a new group of poor whites, still socially segregated from the middle and upper classes. As late as the 1950s the children of mill workers in many places had their own elementary schools, went to separate churches, lived in mill villages, and could not socialize with their schoolmates. As Scout experienced, a middle-class child could not ask a mill village child to her house for an after-school visit.

In Alabama, as in most of the South, the "survival of the caste system," rested upon the assumption that "class distinctions should be rigidly maintained" (Cason, *90° in the Shade*, 30) and continued through the time of *Go Set a Watchman*, even as poor white farmers began moving to urban areas with the hope of making $10 a week in factories.

Social Class in *To Kill a Mockingbird*

Several classes populate the Maycomb, Alabama, area. Jem, in his wisdom, pins the matter down. There are all the black people; the shiftless class, "down at the dump," represented by the Ewells; the Old Sarum farmers like the Cunninghams who work hard but can't afford essentials like shoes for their children; and the middle class of town merchants and professionals like Atticus. Atticus calls his class the common folk, though he would also use the term "common" in a derogatory way in scolding Scout for using a racial slur. What Jem doesn't mention in his four categories are those like Aunt Alexandra who believe their ancestry places them at the top. Each group looks down on those beneath them. Some of the divides have to do with money and many with race. There are admirable and not so admirable people in most categories; nevertheless, the portraits of lower-class whites in *To Kill a Mockingbird* are largely negative.

Lower Class

Early in her school life, Scout believes that there is a "caste system" in Maycomb, made up of older people and ordinary people. After Tom Robinson's trial Scout complicates the definition of class by suggesting that it depends on whether you can read or write. Scout finally concludes that there is only one kind of folks, just folks. Jem rejects this because, if they were all just folks, why wouldn't they get along? Why would they despise each other as they do?

Matters of class, as distinct from race, in *To Kill a Mockingbird* focus primarily on the two lowest classes of poor whites. Scout and Atticus defend the Cunninghams as decent people, but it is from these two lower classes that most of the heartless, catastrophic events arise: false charges of rape, the attempted lynching, the unjust jury decision, and the attempted murder of the children. They are outsiders and, in Maycomb, we see them from the perspective of the middle class. They have different cultures, different language, different attire, and different habits from the white middle class.

The first mention of class is in Boo's history. He gets in trouble as a teenager through his involvement with a troublesome "gang" of Cunningham boys from Old Sarum who were derided from the pulpit because they "hung out in barbershops," went to dances in "the county's riverside gambling hell," enjoyed the fishing camps, and "experimented with stumphold whiskey." One night the gang gets too rowdy and rambunctious, resists arrest, locks up the law-enforcing "beadle" in the courthouse outhouse, and so are sentenced to a state industrial school. Boo, who like the other boys may have received a good education there, is instead locked inside his father's house for a lifetime.

The earliest scenes of the book develop Scout's multiple encounters with Old Sarum children on the first day of school. They begin when her young, inexperienced teacher from northern Alabama, knowing nothing of their town dynamics, quizzes Walter Cunningham about why he has no lunch. Walter is the only child not to put a lunch on his desk. His physical appearance identifies his class: "Walter Cunningham's face told everyone in the first grade he had hookworms. His absence of shoes told us how he got them. . . . He did have on a clean shirt and neatly mended overalls." Scout is called upon by the other students to explain Walter's situation. Instead of beginning with the truth that Walter would never be able to afford to bring lunch, even if he was able to continue appearing, she tries to educate the teacher about Walter's father's ethics, that Cunninghams would never take gifts or charity from anyone, even in these hard times of the Depression. The reason Scout knows this is because Walter's father had slowly but surely paid Atticus for legal services with farm produce over the course of a year. Atticus had explained at the time that the Depression had hit people like the Cunninghams the hardest. Their land was heavily mortgaged and the little money they made was needed to pay interest. He also explained that Mr. Cunningham might be able to get a job with the WPA—the Works Progress Administration set up by President Franklin Roosevelt—but it would mean he would not have time to maintain his land, which he did not want to go to ruin. Other professionals, like Atticus, were paid in produce. For example, Dr. Reynolds received a bushel of potatoes in exchange for delivering a baby, something that Scout will bring up later to Walter.

When Scout explains that the reason Walter can't take Miss Caroline's quarter is because he can never pay it back, Miss Caroline "pats" her hand with a ruler in punishment and makes her stand in the corner.

Scout, who blames Walter for her punishment, catches him in the schoolyard and starts beating him up until Jem stops her and finds out her grievance, looks at Walter, and invites him to noon dinner, telling him that "Our daddy's a friend of your daddy's."

The burdens of being a member of the Old Sarum class become apparent as Walter explains at lunch that he can't pass first grade because he must work in the fields, and when, to the astonishment of Scout, he pours syrup over his vegetables and meat.

Back at school, the misfortunes of the lower class are again emphasized. Little Chuck Little, "another member of the population who didn't know where his next meal was coming from," was, nevertheless, a "true gentleman" who tries to calm down, comfort, and educate Miss Caroline after she sees lice coming from the head of Burris Ewell. Burris is even beneath the other lower-class white students: "His neck was dark gray, the backs of his hands were rusty, and his fingernails were black deep into the quick" (27). Burris is definitely seen as a member of a class separate from other poor whites. "Whole school's full of them."

Atticus enlarges on the Ewells' class. When Scout, who hates school, objects that it isn't fair that Burris Ewell doesn't have to go to school after the first day, yet she has to, Atticus again has to explain a social reality of Maycomb—the lawless Ewells, ranked beneath the Cunninghams for generations because they avoided all honest work, lived like animals. "Atticus said the Ewells had been the disgrace of Maycomb for three generations. None of them had done an honest day's work in his recollection" (30).

The jury is inevitably made up of the same kind of lower-class farmers that tried to lynch Tom. This happens because townspeople would always get out of jury duty for business or social reasons. Even the judge in the cases before him stereotypes the Old Sarum farmers.

The trial brings on the scene the adult Ewells at the bottom of the white social ranking. Their abode is deliberately contrasted with the neatly swept yards of the nearby black community where Tom Robinson's family lives. They live by the dump in a shack once abandoned by black tenants. Their filthy yard is full of junk:

> The cabin's plank walls were supplemented with sheets of corrugated iron, its roof shingled with tin cans hammered flat. . . . [T]he cabin rested uneasily upon four irregular lumps of limestone. . . . what passed for a fence was bits of tree-limbs, broomsticks and tool shafts. . . . Enclosed in this barricade was a dirty yard containing the remains of a Model-T Ford (on blocks), a discarded dentist's chair, an ancient icebox, plus lesser items, old

shoes, worn-out table radios, picture frames, and fruit jars, under which scrawny orange chickens pecked hopefully. (170)

Although this is the only family introduced by the narrator of such low rank, Lee writes: "Every town the size of Maycomb had families like the Ewells. No economic fluctuations changed their status. In good and bad economic times, they lived off the county" (170). Nothing could tame their lawlessness—truant officers or public health officers. They suffered from diseases and worms that came from their filthy environment. Ewell, himself, volunteers that he had never had the services of a doctor for himself or his many children.

Mayella Ewell has absorbed her lowly rank so completely that she thinks when Atticus addresses her as "Miss Mayella" and "ma'am" he is making fun of her—"mockin'" her.

Tom, in his testimony, unconsciously stresses her lowly rank and enrages all the whites present, including the Old Sarum jury, when he confesses that he helped Mayella because he felt sorry for her.

After the trial, Jem and Atticus discuss the jury, made up primarily of dirt-poor farmers—"those folks," according to Jem, who are in a different class from the Finches, who had been part of the lynch mob the night before. On a positive note regarding citizens of Old Sarum, Atticus suspects that Mr. Cunningham has persuaded his double first cousin on the jury to argue (unsuccessfully) against finding Tom guilty. In gratitude, Scout plans to invite Walter to dinner again and maybe even to spend the night. She has not counted on the class intolerance of her Aunt Alexandra: "I still say that Jean Louise will not invite Walter Cunningham to this house. If he were her double first cousin once removed he would still not be received in this house unless he comes to see Atticus on business. Now that is that. . . . Because—he—is—trash, that's why you can't play with him" (224, 225). Aunt Alexandra's rant leads to the children's discussion of class cited earlier.

Some readers have criticized the work for stereotyping not only black people, but low-class whites as well. Historian Wayne Flynt, for example, in his iconic *Poor But Proud*, a history of poor whites in Alabama, cites *To Kill a Mockingbird* as an example of fiction giving "poor whites no respite," and relying on "familiar stereotypes" (214).

Middle and Upper Class

The crowd that appears at the Finches' front door after Atticus agrees to defend Tom Robinson calls attention to another level, another social rank—the middle class of professionals and merchants—Mr. Underwood (the newspaper editor); their neighbor, Mr. Avery; Dr. Reynolds, a physician; and in-town farmers. They justify their gathering as expressing their concern for what the lower-class farmers ("that Old Sarum bunch") might do to hurt Atticus or someone else when they get drunk. Yet, it is telling that Jem fears the crowd of these "respectable" people and manages to disperse them by calling Atticus to the telephone.

The crowd is proven right shortly thereafter when a drunken Old Sarum mob gathers with the purpose of dragging Tom from his jail cell, lynching him, and hurting Atticus in the process if they must. They are described as a different order of persons from the crowd who approached the Finch house the night before. Their lower-class position is made clear: Scout notices: "There was a smell of stale whiskey and pigpen about, and when I glanced around I discovered that these men were strangers. They were not the people I saw last night" (152). Atticus has a somewhat innocent and conflicting description of them, calling them a gang of wild animals, but insisting that the children try to understand that they are still human.

The middle-class whites who travel to the courthouse on the day of the trial are not the dangerous Old Sarum types intent on lynching, but they are scarcely charitable, dignified, or intelligent in their judgment of Atticus's role as a dedicated defender of Tom Robinson.

The definition of class comes up again in the children's conversation about Dolphus Raymond who Dill automatically labels as "trash" because he lives with black people. But Raymond cannot be so labeled because, despite this and his appearance, he is upper class because he owns lots of land and comes from an old family.

Ancestry

Aunt Alexandra introduces the idea of the privileged class in *To Kill a Mockingbird* by preaching about her obsessions with ancestry and background. "She never let a chance escape her to point out the shortcomings of other tribal groups to the greater glory of our own" (129). We have already seen her insistence that Scout become a lady—something that an Old Sarum girl or Mayella Ewell could never be because of her class. When Alexandra moves to Maycomb, she becomes a social leader in, even a symbol of, upper-class society. Her refreshments served at the missionary society are cherished and she becomes secretary of the fancy Maycomb Amanuenis Club. She is very "family" conscious and explains her "preoccupation" with heredity, meaning the Finches' gentle upper-class ranking. Unlike Scout, Aunt Alexandra defines fine people as those who had been landed gentry, living on their land the longest. Jem counters that that would include the Ewells, who had been living by the dump for a very long time. Atticus good-naturedly taunts her with the habit in the distant past of their ancestors of marrying their cousins. When she boasts about their Cousin Joshua, an upper-class poet, the other Finches think of Joshua's attempted murder of the University of Alabama president, a fact she chooses to ignore. Finally Atticus is compelled to have a private talk with the children to explain his sister's motives:

> Your aunt has asked me to try and impress upon you and Jean Louise that you are not from run-of-the-mill people, that you are the product of several generations' gentle breeding . . . and that you should try to live up to your name— . . . She asked me to tell you you must try to behave like the little lady and gentleman you are. She wants to talk to you about the family and what it means to Maycomb County through the years, so you'll have some idea of who you are. (133)

From this the reader surmises that a good part of the reason for Aunt Alexandra's deserting her own family to move in with Atticus seems to be to bring the children to realize and perpetuate their aristocratic background. But Atticus ends up joking about it.

The epitome of the upper middle class at the top of Maycomb society is the Missionary Society, church-going families whom Aunt Alexandra does not consider to be "trash," and are therefore allowed into the Finch house. Miss Maudie, hearing their intolerant comments about black people and Atticus's defense of a black man, redefines people with true "background": "The handful of people in this town who say that fair play is not marked White Only; the handful of people who say a fair trial is for everybody, not just us; the handful of people with enough humility to think, when they look at a Negro, there but for the Lord's kindness am I. . . . The handful of people in town with background" (236).

Social Class in *Go Set a Watchman*

Social rank is also a topic of significance in *Go Set a Watchman*, though the Ewells are not mentioned at all, and the "Old Sarum" residents are present primarily in memory only. The real focus here is on the conflict between Aunt Alexandra's old-fashioned upper-class views and Henry Clinton's working-class background. The topic comes up on the train home even before Jean Louise gets to town, as she contemplates her Aunt

Alexandra. She does not look forward to the inevitable conversation about background and Cousin Joshua, who ended up in an institution "for the irresponsible" (5).

The genteel Joshua St. Clair is the opposite of Henry Clinton. Jean Louise sees Henry, as she comes into town, as one of "her own kind," although he is the son of the area's poor whites. Even before they reach the Finch house, just after he picks her up from the train station, the reader is provided with Hank's history. His father, probably an alcoholic, deserted the family, and his mother worked in a store in what might be described as a blue-collar job, struggling to put Hank through public school. From the age of twelve, he boarded across the street from the Finches, and "this in itself put him on a higher plane" (12). At 14 his mother died and he was forced to work in a fast-food franchise to support himself. Then he joined the army, and, finally, with Atticus's help, finished law school at the University of Alabama.

The central conflict over class begins when Jean Louise raises the prospect to her aunt of a marriage to Henry, whom she has known for years and dated and who is Atticus's right-hand man. Her aunt responds that though he is the finest boy she knows, his background makes him unsuitable to marry a Finch and that Atticus would not be happy with it.

> Jean Louise, dating a boy is one thing, but marrying him's another. You must take all things into account. Henry's background— . . . Henry is not and never will be suitable for you. We Finches do not marry the children of rednecked white trash, which is exactly what Henry's parents were when they were born and were all their lives. . . . Fine a boy as he is, the trash won't wash out of him. (34, 36, 37)

She proceeds to list four of his personal habits that prove he is not right for Jean Louise, after each one saying "Trash," a word that will continue to pop up throughout the novel.

After this contretemps, before Jean Louise and Hank go out on their first date since she got home for vacation, she says she is "closer to marrying trash than she'd ever been in her life" (39). When she relays to him that Aunt Alexandra doesn't approve of him, he replies that he's always known that.

At the White Citizens' Council meeting, she can see for herself ways in which social ranks have shifted. There sitting at the table with her father is one William Willoughby, a crooked county powerhouse she thought Atticus hated. Willoughby, a man whose "life blood was poverty" has risen to great influential heights in Maycomb and controlled something not unlike a local mafia. Yet a powerful issue that has brought white men from every class together for this meeting is the fear that black men will be elected to and corrupt public office.

One white man who is not there is one of the Old Sarum Cunninghams whom Scout runs into after fleeing the Maycomb Citizens' Council meeting. His mother had left him enough timberland to allow him to buy a business in the village.

Jean Louise's memories take her back to school in Maycomb where her friends were not the children of the town's elite, but those of working-class and poor farmers of Old Sarum. She took to the newcomers immediately—new to her in sixth grade because their own school had burned down. The earliest days in school that year were the happiest because of them, especially the rough boys. She played craps and chewed tobacco with the boys and chose the Old Sarum girls for the girls' volleyball team. The girls explained and comforted her when menstruation began and inadvertently led her astray about the facts of life, which caused her to become convinced that she was pregnant.

Naturally, none of her Old Sarum girlfriends are among those at Aunt Alexandra's coffee party, only grownups who refused Scout's company when they were little. Class bias comes up when Hester talks about the possibility of black people seducing white people. When Jean Louise objects, Hester misunderstands and says, "Jean Louise, when I said that I wasn't referring to *us* . . . I was talking about the—you know, the trashy people."

The powerful implications of social rank or class come to a head in Jean Louise's discussion with Hank after she has found him supporting the Maycomb Citizens' Council. She tells him she can never marry someone who shares the attitudes and goals of such a racist group, no matter how "respectable" they are. He answers that he has to be part of this racist core of the community because he is a low-class white. First he reminds her of what she already knows, that he has had to "work like a dog for everything I ever had," ever since he was a little boy, coming home from work, "so tired most of the time it was all I could do to keep up with my lessons." He reminds her that she has grown up a privileged Finch and so is free to behave any way she likes. For him it is different. "But let Henry Clinton show any signs of deviatin' from the norm and Maycomb says, not 'That's the Clinton in him,' but 'That's the trash in him'" (232). Still somehow Jean Louise believes that Hank is using his class as an excuse for participating in the racism of the community. She calls him on his listing of his ambitions, putting money first and a wife last.

The discussion of class in the novel ends with Uncle Jack telling her, regarding Hank, that "He's not your kind." Jean Louise thinks he is raising Aunt Alexandra's background issues again and says, "Look, I'm not going to argue with you over the relative merits of trash—" (272). He corrects her, implying his objection to Hank is something else. "That has nothing to do with it. I'm tired of you" (273). Uncle Jack's view of "our kind" may be closer to Jean Louise's own.

Further Reading

Cash, W. J. *The Mind of the South*. New York: Vintage Books, 1969.

Cason, Clarence. *90° in the Shade*. 1935. Reprint. Tuscaloosa: University of Alabama Press, 1983.

Davis, Allison, Burleigh B. Gardner, and Mary R. Gardner. *Deep South: A Social Anthropological Study of Caste and Class*. Chicago: University of Chicago Press, 1941.

Davis, Allison, Burleigh B. Gardner, and Mary R. Gardner. *Deep South: A Social Anthropological Study of Caste and Class*. With a new introduction by Jennifer Jensen Wallach. Columbia: University of South Carolina Press, 2009.

Flynt, Wayne. *Alabama in the Twentieth Century*. Tuscaloosa: University of Alabama Press, 2004.

Flynt, Wayne. *Poor But Proud: Alabama's Poor Whites*. Tuscaloosa: University of Alabama Press, 1989.

Grafton, Carl, and Anne Permaloff. *Big Mules and Branchheads: James E. Folsom and Political Power in Alabama*. Athens: University of Georgia Press, 1985.

Hackney, Sheldon. *Populism to Progressive in Alabama*. Princeton, NJ: Princeton University Press, 1969.

Hamilton, Virginia Van der Veer. *Alabama: A Bicentennial History*. New York: W. W. Norton, 1977.

Isenberg, Nancy. *White Trash: The 400-Year Untold History of Class in America*. New York: Penguin Books, 2016.

Lee, Harper. *Go Set a Watchman*. New York: HarperCollins, 2015.

Lee, Harper. *To Kill a Mockingbird*. Philadelphia: J. B. Lippincott, 1960. Warner Books paperback edition, 1982.

Phelps, Teresa Godwin. "The Margins of Maycomb: A Rereading of *To Kill a Mockingbird*." *Alabama Law Review* 45, no. 2 (Winter 1994): 511–30.

Tindall, George Brown. *The Emergence of the New South 1913–1945*. Baton Rouge: Louisiana State University Press, 1967.

CHAPTER SEVEN

The South

The setting of both *To Kill a Mockingbird* and *Go Set a Watchman* is the Deep South: its character and how Scout/Jean Louise comes to terms with it is the subject. Questions of race, gender, and the gothic in the South have been explored in earlier chapters. This chapter will search more deeply into images of the South, how it changes over time, and how Jean Louise reacts to the New South.

The action of *Go Set a Watchman* is primarily intellectual and emotional, as Jean Louise determines whether she will return to the South to live or return to her home in New York City. She realizes always, even up to the end of the novel, that the South is her inherited home. It is where she was born, where her family is, where she went to school, where she and her brother developed together, and where she learned so many things (like the expression ring-tailed son of a bitch!). She wonders as she is on the train "why she had never thought her country beautiful" (6). When she waxes sentimental about Finch's Landing, her boyfriend, Hank, in reference to *Gone With the Wind*, says, "Going Southern on us? Want me to do a Gerald O'Hara?" (74).

Atticus knows that if Jean Louise were home permanently, she would be miserable. Except for Atticus (who has sent her away in the first place to become her own person), though, people she meets ask her why she won't move back South. Aunt Alexandra has been making her feel guilty about it for years. "I do think, Jean Louise, that now is the time for you to come home for good" becomes a tiresome, maddening refrain. Even Mr. Fred the grocer complicates things for her as he tells the story of his leaving and returning to Maycomb: "Why don't you stay home this time? . . . You never get it out of your bones" (153). Hank, of course, proposes marriage several times and her acceptance would mean she would have to move back South. Even Uncle Jack, who seems to understand so much, tries to make an argument for her return: "Well, at the risk of overloading you, could you possibly give an understanding to think about it?" (272). He tells her that the South needs her and that there are more people of her kind in the South than she realizes.

It is the South that is on trial in *Go Set a Watchman*, and though there have been different interpretations of what Jean Louise will finally do, the text (and Nelle Harper Lee's own personal decision) support the conclusion that the South loses at trial and, though Jean Louise completes her ten-day vacation stay, she then returns to New York City for good.

It is useful to look at the portrayal of the South in both novels, written at about the same time.

Mrs. Dubose as Symbol of the Antebellum South

Mrs. Henry Lafayette Dubose, whose very name suggests the antebellum aristocracy, is a formative presence in the lives of Jem and Scout in *To Kill a Mockingbird*. She is clearly a representative of the Old South. One of the first things the reader learns about her—and that is repeatedly referenced—is that she is connected to the Confederacy and its violence. She is rumored to keep a Confederate States of America pistol hidden under her shawls and wraps, even when she is sitting on her porch. Atticus angers Scout for sending Jem to talk to Mrs. Dubose alone for fear that his only son would be "murdered with a Confederate relic"—a term that has a double meaning: her gun and herself.

The second Old South connection is her yard full of white camellias with which she is obsessed. After Jem cuts them down with a baton, they have to be recultivated. She sends one to Jem when she is dying. Her camellias are not just a personal preference: they are a historical reference to the Old South during Reconstruction and just afterward. The Knights of the Order of the White Camellia sprang up in 1867 in Louisiana, founded, as was the Ku Klux Klan, with which it shared values, by a Confederate Army veteran. While the Ku Klux Klan was largely made up of lower-class whites, the Knights of the White Camellia was a secret upper-class organization that flourished in the South. The color (or noncolor) is of significance here. The founder's name was deBlanc, and the flower stood for "pure" white society. Christopher Long, in the *Handbook of Texas*, describes its platform: "Its members were pledged to support the supremacy of the white race, to oppose the amalgamation of the races, to resist the social and political encroachment of the carpetbaggers, and to restore white control of the government."

Mrs. Dubose could very well be a supporter of the Knights of the White Camellia with her racist terrorism from her front porch. She is the first adult the children hear yelling racist slurs concerning their father's defense of Tom Robinson. She lets the children know that their father is no better than the black people and the "trash he works for," and that he is going "against his raising" (102). Like a student of the Old South, she is obsessed with proper "manners," correcting Scout's greeting and, like others, criticizing her attire.

One of the most intriguing connections between Mrs. Dubose and the Old South is that Jem must read Sir Walter Scott's *Ivanhoe* to her out loud as punishment for vandalizing her flowers. Both novelist and novel were idolized by the gentry of the South. Scott perpetuated shallow romance and superficial values: sectionalism, clannishness (is this where "Klan" came from?), emphasis on appearance and manners, a distorted sense of honor that resulted in deadly duels over "an insult," and a tradition of ladies and knights. Remember the word "Knight" in the racist organization. Mark Twain, though he seemed to like the writer, once declared that Sir Walter Scott had *caused* the Civil War, and in *The Adventures of Huckleberry Finn*, a sinking ship of murderers and robbers is named the *Sir Walter Scott*. W. J. Cash, in his distinguished history of Southern culture, *The Mind of the South*, remarks repeatedly on the connections between the values of the Old South and Sir Walter Scott.

For these reasons there seems to be little doubt that Mrs. Dubose is intended to be a symbol of the Old South. If so, what hints are we given to the character of that time and place? In the first place, she is spoken of as "very old," sick, and crippled. She is "vicious," with a "wrathful" gaze. She is addicted, not just to heroin, but to a hateful point of view. She lies, saying that the Finches are in mental institutions. Her house is dark and creepy and smells bad: "She was horrible. Her face was the color of a dirty pillowcase, and the corners of her mouth glistened with wet, which inched like a glacier down the deep grooves enclosing her chin. . . . Her bottom plate was not in, and her upper lip protruded: . . . From time to time she would open her mouth wide, and I could see her tongue undulate faintly. Cords of saliva would collect on her lips" (106, 107). This is hardly the vision of a Scarlett O'Hara with her dark hair and beautiful face sitting on her veranda at Tara, surrounded by beaus, in *Gone With the Wind*.

Like others in the South, Mrs. Dubose is fascinated by the past—*Ivanhoe* and old families. Names here illuminate a particular narrative view of the antebellum South, represented by Mrs. Dubose. The worthless, rapist, would-be child murderer villain of the novel is named for the commander of the Confederate Army: "Robert E. Lee" Ewell. Editor Underwood, prepared to save Atticus from the lynch mob, but who hates black people, is also named for a Confederate general—Braxton Bragg. Atticus jokes that people named for Confederate generals were slow and steady drinkers.

Aunt Alexandra: A Symbol of the Elite South

In both *To Kill a Mockingbird* and *Go Set a Watchman*, Aunt Alexandra, as we have seen in previous chapters, is an unmistakable representation of what she see as the upper-class Southern belle or matron. In *Go Set a Watchman* she is described as "enarmored, hatted, gloved, perfumed, and ready" for church. She brags that she (and the other Finches) are from rich, landowning, therefore aristocratic, families. She insists on perfectly genteel behavior, and berates Scout for even thinking about marrying "white trash." She demands that her family have nothing to do with blacks or low-class whites, no matter how respectable they are. She becomes enraged in *Go Set a Watchman* when she learns that Jean Louise has visited Calpurnia: "Jean Louise, nobody in Maycomb goes to see Negroes any more, not after what they've been doing to us. Besides being shiftless now they look at you sometimes with open insolence" (166).

Aunt Alexandra is at the center of Maycomb social life, and entertains like the proper Southern hostess: "her Missionary Society refreshment were still the best in town; her activities in Maycomb's three cultural clubs increased." It is Alexandra who is queen at the Missionary Society meeting in *To Kill a Mockingbird* and the snobbish coffee party in *Go Set a Watchman*, both of which groups display, not only racism, but in the coffee party, at least, the trivia and constraints within which Southern women live.

What is Jean Louise's reaction to Aunt Alexandra, this second symbol of the South? She calls her aunt "the enemy" (29), and recalls that Alexandra had made her whole life "hell on wheels" (26). Alexandra and her South can torture Jean Louise and "tweak" her conscience, as with the insistence that Atticus's daughter move back to Maycomb to help take care of him. When her true emotions burst out: "And you, you are a pompous, narrow-minded old—" (258), she has to abjectly apologize to her aunt.

Henry Clinton: A Symbol of the New South

Alexandra represents the gentrified South of Scout's childhood and young womanhood, and Henry ("Hank") Clinton represents the New South of politicians and businessmen. He's the rising lower-class guy with the new car, a law degree, a law partnership, and a fancy Kiwanis Club award. The values that shape his ambition are money, community respect, and political power.

They had known each other as children. He is smart, appealing, witty, a character to whom she is romantically, physically attracted. Marriage to Henry would be marriage to the South and she momentarily considers it, but always tells him no. At first, it is not so much Hank that she consistently rejects as it is marriage.

There are values and priorities beneath Hank's surface that don't dawn on her when she first returns. Primarily, that is Henry's unbounded ambition, at the expense of everything, including what is right. Neither Hank nor the new, industrialized South have a watchman of conscience telling them what is moral and ethical, especially with regard to race.

One hint of Henry's state of mind comes as early as their trip home from the train station when he describes to her how a woman can please a man: hold your tongue, don't argue with him even when you know you're right. "Smile a lot, Make him feel big. Tell him how wonderful he is, and wait on him" (10). This is such an absurd bit of advice for someone like Jean Louise that we initially read it as a joke, but later disclosures prompt the reader to reevaluate it as serious.

Despite Aunt Alexandra's snobbishness, her analysis of Henry, soon after Jean Louise arrives, gives one pause: "he thinks he can make a place for himself in this town by riding on your father's coattails. The very idea, trying to take your father's place in the Methodist Church, trying to take over his law practice, driving all around the country in his car. Why, he acts like this house was his own already. . . . Why, all of Maycomb's talking about Henry Clinton grabbing everything Atticus has—" (37). Although Jean Louise's reaction to her aunt is that she is spewing ugly classism, one has to return to her rant after Scout's afternoon talk with Hank before she confronts Atticus.

At the Landing, Jean Louise kids him about being "a rising young man," as he tells her of his political aspirations. He is part of the changing world, yet the changes after World War II that Jean Louise sees do not please her, as Henry notices when they walk in the restaurant. "You don't like it, do you? . . . I saw your face when you walked in the door" (46). She answers, "The only thing I like about it is the smell is gone." The Maycomb veterans (like Henry) "returned with bizarre ideas about making money and an urgency to make up for lost time" (45).

Jean Louise, an educated young woman, has been exposed to enough news in New York to know what the White Citizens' Council is and to be disturbed by her father's and Henry's participation in Maycomb's version of this organization. Once in the balcony, seeing the two of them sitting at the table and actually hearing the ignorant venom being spewed by their guest speaker, without the slightest objection from Hank or her father, her view of him and the South explodes.

As with the novelist's technique in sketching the coffee party, the substance and tone of the meeting are expressed, not in sentences, but in words or phrases from the speech of their guest, O'Hanlon (a White Citizens' Council representative): "essential inferiority . . . still in the trees . . . take 'em all out and shoot 'em" (108). Immediately after she tries to make sense of it all, of her relationship to the South:

> Had she been able to think, Jean Louise might have prevented events to come by considering the day's occurrences in terms of a recurring story as old as time: the chapter which concerned her began two hundred years ago and was played out in a proud society the bloodiest war and harshest peace in modern history could not destroy. . . .
>
> Had she insight, could she have pierced the barriers of her highly selective, insular world, she may have discovered that all her life she had been with a visual defect . . . : she was born color blind. (122)

She will tell Hank the effect that this turning point in their relationship had on her: "I was at that meeting yesterday. I saw you and Atticus in your glory down there at that table with that—that scum, that dreadful man, and I tell you my stomach turned. Merely the man I was going to marry, merely my own father, merely made me so sick I threw up and haven't stopped yet! How in the name of God could you? How could you?" (228).

Shortly after the White Citizens' Council meeting, in their law office, it is Hank who just assumes that Atticus will not defend Zeebo's son—their "family," as Jean Louise sees it. Hank mistakenly tells the sheriff that Atticus won't "touch" the case.

By the time Jean Louise meets Henry in the cafe, she will cut off her romantic relationship with Henry if not their friendship, and make it clear and final that she won't marry him. The New South he embodies has made her furious. "Right now I can't even speak to him," she thinks (226). It is not just his political point of view that she rejects. He confesses that he thinks a woman, like their friend Hester who is dominated by her husband, has to lose some of her self when she marries. Jean Louise clarifies, "You mean losing your own identity, don't you?" He answers, "In a way, yes." To which she answers, if that is true, she will never marry (227).

Reflecting the pragmatism of the New South, he excuses his participation in the Maycomb Citizens' Council by telling her that "We have to do a lot of things we don't want to do, Jean Louise" (228), in short, whether it is right and ethical or not. She is outraged by this answer. He goes on with the story of his economic ambition: "My bread and butter comes from this town, and Maycomb's given me a good living" (230). He rationalizes further, that, in return, he has to fit in and join the establishment in all its approved forms, including the "respectable" social organizations, such as the church and the White Citizens' Council. He does this, not because it is the right thing to do for himself and the community, but because he is, like the New South, driven by personal ambition. He wants to "make a name for myself" and "I want to make money."

In response, Jean Louise calls him a coward and a hypocrite for not standing up for what is decent. There will be no marriage—period. She comes to the conclusion that the South "had rendered her useless to him as anything other than his oldest friend" (276).

It is obvious that the South, as well, loses the case to keep Jean Louise home. After her breakup with Hank, she thinks of her quandary. This is her home, "But I am not their blood . . . I am a stranger at a cocktail party" (225).

Jean Louise and Maycomb

As a result of her experiences on this vacation, she is often impressed with the fact that these are not her people, as she had once thought they were: "Now she was aware of a sharp apartness, a separation, not from Atticus and Henry merely. All of Maycomb and Maycomb County were leaving her as the hours passed, and she automatically blamed herself" (154).

In *Go Set a Watchman* she remembers her reaction to Maycomb as a child: "Hell was and would always be as far as she was concerned, a lake of fire exactly the size of Maycomb, Alabama, surrounded by a brick wall two hundred feet high" (61).

She knows, especially after the coffee party, that life and marriage in the South would simply be torture for her: "I'd be churched to death, bridge-partied to death, called upon to give book reviews at the Amanuensis Club, expected to become a part of the community. It takes a lot of what I don't have to be a member of this wedding" (173).

Uncle Jack: A Symbol of the Southern Intellectual

In her first long conversation with Uncle Jack, he tries to mollify her with the fact that "men like your father are fighting a sort of rearguard, delaying action to preserve a certain kind of philosophy that's almost gone down the drain—" to which Jean Louise replies, "good riddance" (188, 189). Jack rationalizes Atticus's position by talking about the rise of the lower classes as factory workers, still looking down on black people, the yearning to preserve white civilization, and the threat of a new birth in the South that neither he nor Atticus can stop with the weapon of the White Citizens' Council. Jean Louise keeps saying, why don't you answer me? "Stop woolgathering and answer me!" (200).

In their second conversation, Uncle Jack is successful in calming her down and persuading her to remain for the rest of her vacation but when he makes a brief appeal for her return to live in Maycomb, even though he realizes that Hank is not her kind (not because of his class, but because of his values), her reply is, in effect, no: "Uncle Jack, I can't live in a place that I don't agree with and that doesn't agree with me" (272).

Out of the South: New York

The contrast with the South is New York City where Jean Louise (and at this time, Nelle Harper Lee) have been living for five years. References to the city reverberate in the novel from beginning to end. She sees a lot to criticize about the South throughout her visit but, unlike the Maycomb citizens she encounters, has mostly good things to say about New York.

One of Henry's first questions when he picks her up at the station is whether she is now tired of New York and the answer is a definitive "no." Hank asks her later where she had picked up her sassy wisdom, and she replies, "Living in sin in New York." Aunt Alexandra begins harassing her about her informal clothes, causing Jean Louise to think that one reason she has left her more dressy work clothes behind is to be comfortable on vacation and so Maycomb people won't gossip that she has "gone New York." She knows of the disapproval of her Aunt Alexandra's cousin and beau, Edgar, and says, "'I reckon he thinks my living alone in New York is ipso facto living in sin" (25).

The coffee club attendees who disparage New York (as they had snubbed her when she was a little girl) say, "WELL, HOW'S NEW YORK?" Her thoughts in answer to the question are expansive: "New York. New York? I'll tell you how New York is. New York has all the answers. People go to the YMCA, the English-Speaking Union, Carnegie Hall, the New School for Social Research, and find the answers." This is followed by a mental argument with imagined New Yorkers about who she is and how she should react to the racism in her family. But her spoken answer to the coffee group is "New York? It'll always be there" (179), and thinks again, "I can tell you. In New York you are your own person. You may reach out and embrace all of Manhattan in sweet aloneness, or you can go to hell if you want to" (180).

When talking to Atticus, she thinks of "creeping" back to New York and making all she loved in the South a memory. These people are no longer her own kind. Uncle Jack's argument about bigotry and conscience, while probably not completely satisfactory to the reader, is seen to calm her down and open her eyes about her father and the South. Uncle Jack puts his finger on the real problem: she had confused her father with God; her idol had fallen, and she shortly meets Atticus and welcomes him "silently to the human race" (278).

But, although she will finish up her vacation in harmony with her family, there is little doubt that she will return to New York, the only place she can be free, the only place she can be herself.

Further Reading

Carmer, Carl. *Stars Fell on Alabama*. New York: Doubleday, 1934.

Cash, W. J. *The Mind of the South*. New York: Alfred A. Knopf, 1941.

Cason, Clarence. *90° in the Shade*. 1935. Reprint. Tuscaloosa: University of Alabama Press, 1983.

Cobb, James C. *The Selling of the South: The Southern Crusade for Industrial Development, 1936–1980*. Baton Rouge: Louisiana State University Press, 1982.

Faulkner, William. "A Rose for Emily." In *The Portable Faulkner*. New York: Viking Press, 1946.

Lee, Harper. *Go Set a Watchman*. New York: HarperCollins, 2015.

Lee, Harper. *To Kill a Mockingbird*. Philadelphia: J. B. Lippincott, 1960. Warner Books paperback edition, 1982.

Long, Christopher. "Knights of the White Camellia." *Handbook of Texas*. Texas State Historical Association. https://tshaonline.org/handbook/online/articles/vek01.

Saul, Stephanie. "Edging Out of a Confederate Shadow, Gingerly." *New York Times*, August 10, 2017, A10.

Wyatt-Brown, Bertram. *The Shaping of Southern Culture: Honor, Grace, and War*. Chapel Hill: University of North Carolina Press, 2001.

CHAPTER EIGHT

The Hero: Atticus Finch

Over fifty years after the publication of *To Kill a Mockingbird*, the question of heroism, especially the heroism of the civilian (as opposed to that of the professional soldier), continues to be an issue. Although in earlier times there might have been little debate over Atticus's heroism, in the late 1980s and 1990s history began being revised. Previously accepted ideas about ethics and ultimate meaning have been reexamined and overturned, often in light of more recent interpretations of motives and our reexamination of public figures. Heroes are suddenly found wanting when they are measured against the social and moral view of an age not their own.

The question of what constitutes a hero like Atticus Finch arose in a time when Americans looked back on civilian citizens of the 1950s and 1960s, both black and white, who performed heroic actions, for example, in the civil rights struggle, and those who suffered as a result of their heroism. Many of these courageous people were lawyers and judges like Atticus Finch. And, coming into print at the height of the civil rights struggle was *To Kill a Mockingbird*, a novel that first gave the world the image of the courageous Southern attorney and that subsequently became a popular film.

To Kill a Mockingbird

For many readers, the Atticus of *To Kill a Mockingbird* is the ultimate hero. He has opened the eyes of many young Southerners about the racism of their region and inspired numerous young men and women to follow the professions of law or public service. James Carville, a Louisiana-born, well-known public servant in Washington, indicated that the book and the character of Atticus changed his view of life as a young man. One of the most surprising testimonials came from Johnnie Cochran, the black defense attorney, known for his participation in the O. J. Simpson trial. In a column on books in the *California Lawyer*, Cochran chose to write on *To Kill a Mockingbird*: "In my life I encountered one book that resonated deeply with me, and its message became a friendly companion as I embarked upon my journey to justice. This book's effect was so profound that I did not realize its full strength until many years after my initial reading."

The Classic Hero

The classic hero is one who fights with all his might even though he knows he is going to lose. Our modern idea of the hero is usually someone like Atticus who takes a courageous stand against all odds, usually against the establishment, for something he or she believes is right. Heroes put things they value most on the line to accomplish their goals: their reputations, their good names in the community, their careers, their safely, their very lives.

The reader knows Atticus is a decent man, a wise and loving father, a caring neighbor even before his acts of public heroism occur. Miss Maudie tells Scout that Atticus, even if he were a drunk (which he's not) would be a finer person than the self-righteous preachers who harass her because of her flowers. He makes little Walter Cunningham feel welcome and encourages him to talk about his situation. Time after time, he makes humane and sensible decisions with regard to his family. He allows Jem and Scout to follow their own identities, letting Scout wear her overalls and play as she wants to. He reads to them, and talks to them as if they were adults. He makes a bargain, a "compromise," with Scout when her first-grade teacher orders her not to read anymore. "If you'll concede the necessity of going to school, we'll go on reading every night just as we always have" (31). But he firmly draws a line when the children do something hurtful to others, interfering in a controlled and reasonable way, as, for example, when they perform their Boo dramas for all to see: "putting his life's history on display for the edification of the neighborhood" (49). And he is firm in directing them to stop making fun of Mr. Avery with their snowman.

His often quoted advice to his children when they complain about others is to see the situation from the other person's point of view, to climb into the other person's skin, whether it's a sibling, or Mrs. Dubose, or the Cunninghams, or even Bob Ewell. "You never really understand a person until you consider things from his point of view . . . until you climb into his skin and walk around in it" (30). In all things he is reasonable, compassionate, unassuming, honest, and understanding. When Scout comes home using a racial slur she has learned at school, he corrects her: "That's common." And when she insists that everyone else says it, he tells her that now there will be everybody less one.

When Scout further asks him about the racial slurs she is hearing at school, he carefully explains the case to her—that he will be defending a Negro. He enlarges on Tom's excellent character and warns her that she will hear talk around town from people who don't think he should be defending Tom. Scout asks him why he is doing what people don't think he should do, and he explains, "The main one [reason] is, if I didn't I couldn't hold up my head in town. I couldn't represent this county in the legislature. I couldn't even tell you and Jem not to do something again" (76). With Scout curled up in his lap, he says that this time, they are not fighting the Yankees, "we're fighting our friends" (76).

Uncle Jack, after hearing how difficult this trial is going to be for Atticus, makes a reference to Jesus's prayer to God when it becomes clear that he is about to be crucified. "Let this cup pass from you, eh?" (88). Shortly, to the children's astonishment, Atticus try to emulate a savior.

The children, thinking of the physical heroism of warriors and athletes, don't fully appreciate their father's heroism at first. He's an old fifty. "Our father didn't do anything. He worked in an office, not a drugstore. Atticus did not drive a dump-truck for the county, he was not the sheriff, he did not farm, work in a garage, or do anything that could possibly arouse the admiration of anyone. . . . He never went hunting, he did not play poker or fish or drink or smoke. He sat in the living room and read" (89).

Atticus, because those who knew him as a youth realize that he is a crack shot and is the most capable person in the community to face such a dangerous task, is called upon to shoot a mad dog wandering down the street. His children are stunned. "Jem was paralyzed. I pinched him to get him moving" (96). Then: "Jem became vaguely articulate: 'd'you see him, Scout? d'you see him standing there? . . . 'n' all of a sudden he just relaxed all over, an' it looked like that gun was a part of him'" (97).

Miss Maudie, grinning "wickedly," taunts Scout about her former complaint that Atticus couldn't do anything. His nickname when he was a boy, she informs them, was Ol' One-Shot. In answer to Jem who wonders why Atticus doesn't hunt anymore, given his talent, Miss Maudie sums up Atticus's heroic character: "If your father's anything, he's civilized at heart. . . . I think maybe he put his gun down when he realized that God had given him an unfair advantage over most living things. . . . People in their right mind never take pride in their talents" (98).

Atticus's bravery is again in evidence in Scout's mind when he actually greets and chats with the old witch, Mrs. Dubose. "It was times like these when I thought my father, who hated guns and had never been to any wars, was the bravest man who ever lived" (100).

Atticus's bravery is shown when he reminds the town's leaders, who surround his front door, of the truth of Tom Robinson's situation—a truth that they don't want to hear. When he tells them and the sheriff that they know what the truth is, the crowd begins murmuring "ominously" and moves toward him.

Later, his facing off of the lynch mob is one of his most heroic acts, putting himself in danger by deliberately going to the courthouse at night and placing himself alone as a guard outside Tom's jail window, refusing to move away as ordered. Again he faces mad dogs in the street, but this time without a gun.

The next day, as the crowd is gathering for the trial to begin, we hear the townspeople's real objection to Atticus. They realize he was appointed to defend Tom, but that doesn't mean he really has to take his job seriously and actually defend him, which Atticus is doing. Other lawyers would simply go through the motions.

During a break in the trial, Dolphus Raymond and Scout discuss Atticus's character. It begins when Scout quotes Atticus as saying that "cheatin' a colored man is ten times worse than cheatin' a white man. . . . Says it's the worst thing you can do" (201). Dolphus, now an outsider, tells her: "Miss Jean Louise, you don't know your pa's not a run-of-the-mill man, it'll take a few years for that to sink in—you haven't seen enough of the world yet" (201). The recognition of Atticus's heroism, especially on the part of the black citizens, occurs when all the black people in the balcony rise in honor of Atticus as he walks out of the courtroom—as the strongest lines in the novel are spoken by Reverend Sykes, "Miss Jean Louise, stand up. Your father's passin'" (211).

After the verdict is announced, finding Tom guilty, Atticus's life and family are still in serious danger from Bob Ewell, and he is still vilified by the white community.

Despite Atticus's unquestioned times of heroism, there are moments when he betrays a certain naiveté about his own white neighbors. One of them is his conviction, expressed to the men in his front yard, that the Old Sarum residents will not attempt a lynching on Sunday, the day before the trial: "'Don't be foolish, Heck . . . This is Maycomb . . .—besides,' Atticus was saying, 'you're not scared of that crowd, are you? . . . They don't usually drink on Sunday, they go to church most of the day'" (145). He also expressed the belief that the Ku Klux Klan was not a matter for concern. When Jem compares the Klan to a mob, Atticus tells him that he is confusing the Klan of the 1920s with that of their own day in the 1930s. "But," he says, "it was a political organization more than anything. Besides they couldn't find anybody to scare. . . . The Ku Klux's is gone," said Atticus. "It'll never come back." (147). He is also oblivious to the evidence that he and his children are in serious danger from Bob Ewell, despite Ewell's stated intent of revenge, his spitting on Atticus, harassing of the judge, and stalking of Tom Robinson's widow. Just after the trial, even the children and Aunt Alexandra sense the real peril their father is in: "When a man says he's gonna get you, looks like he means it." He tells them there is nothing to be afraid of. "What on earth could Ewell do to me, sister?" She say that it will be something "furtive" (218). On Halloween the children are allowed to go to a school pageant by themselves in the dark, and that night Ewell tries to kill them as they come home.

At the end, Atticus concedes to the sheriff, who had arrested an obviously innocent black man, but now insists on not arresting and investigating an obviously guilty white man for murder. This concession on the part of a man for whom the law has been the preeminent ethic, has struck some readers the wrong way and put Atticus's heroism in question (Lester interview).

Public Perception and Reception of Atticus

Two of the most amazing references to Atticus came from two of the most famous black men in American history: Martin Luther King Jr. and President Barack Obama. King writes of Atticus's heroism in *Why We Can't Wait*: "To the Negro in 1963, as to Atticus Finch, it had become obvious that nonviolence could symbolize the gold badge of heroism rather than the white feather of cowardice." President Obama, in his farewell address to the nation on January 10, 2017, mentions the strength of Atticus's repeated philosophy: "If our democracy is to work in this increasingly diverse nation, each one of us must try to heed the advice of one of the great characters in American fiction, Atticus Finch, who said, 'You never really understand a person until you consider things from his point of view . . . until you climb into his skin and walk around in it.'"

Thomas Shaffer in the *University of Pittsburgh Law Review* offered the typical lawyer's tribute to Atticus as the gentleman/lawyer who instinctively acts admirably because, through the years, proper ethics have become a part of his character. Monroe Freedman quotes other lawyers

who praise Atticus. One from the *ABA Journal* (October 1991): "For me
. . . there is no more compelling role model than Atticus Finch. . . . Fine
citizen, parent and lawyer. Finch . . . would remind us that this burden
[of meeting a higher standard of behavior and trust] is never too much to
bear." Another of Freedman's quotes come from the *Stanford Law Review*
of 1990: "He is a moral character in a world where the role of moral
thought has become at best highly ambivalent."

But Monroe Freedman also fired the first shot, questioning if the Atticus of *To Kill a Mockingbird* was a perfect character or a perfect role model
for lawyers. Freedman brings up the point that Atticus lives in a segregated, unjust world that he seems to accept and do nothing to change.
"The lawyers we should hold up as role models are those who earn their
living in the kinds of practices that most lawyers pursue . . . but who also
volunteer a small but significant amount of their time and skills to advance
social justice. That is the cause that Atticus Finch, a gentleman of character, chose to ignore throughout his legal career" (20).

More recently in a July 2015 book review, Catherine Nichols agreed
with Freedman that Atticus had always been a racist in *To Kill a Mockingbird.* He goes along with a system that had no interest in changing its
practices of discrimination and injustice, nor in investigating the deaths
of a black man (Tom) and a poor man (Ewell). Atticus also seems to identify his politics with a real white supremacist politician from Alabama,
Cotton Tom Heflin.

On February 24, 1992, Freedman opened his column in *Legal Times* by
acknowledging that even though Atticus Finch is fictional, he is mythical,
even immortal. He went on to inform the paper's readers of the reaction to
his criticism of Atticus, declaring that in the two years of writing his very
controversial column, he had never received such outraged objections as
he had to the column criticizing Atticus Finch. He concluded by saying
that readers of his column responded as if he were attacking Mother
Teresa, Gandhi, God, and Bambi all at once. One point in Atticus's favor is
that his defense of Tom Robinson is very difficult, because he has so much
to lose. A more liberal or radical lawyer like the New Yorker who defended
the Scottsboro defendants would find defending Tom much less problem-
atic and psychologically less burdensome than it was for Atticus, an action,
as he says, that puts him at war with his own people to do what is right.

Go Set a Watchman

All the attention of readers, would-be readers, and reviewers of *Go Set a
Watchman* has been almost entirely on Atticus. What can only be described

as the explosive reaction to the novel has been prompted by what people have seen as the shocking, inexplicable differences between the two Atticuses of the two novels—the idol of *To Kill a Mockingbird* and the racist of *Go Set a Watchman*. As Megan Garber wrote in *The Atlantic*, the Atticuses of the two novels represent competing cosmologies, opposite views of race and justice.

Off the Pedestal: Questioning the Hero Narrative

The old Atticus is an uncomplaining seventy-two-year-old man with debilitating arthritis, who nevertheless retains a law office and his business. But most of what is presented of Atticus in *Go Set a Watchman* has to do with his politics. When we first see him, he is looking at a recent (1953) book by William Allen Jowitt, *The Strange Case of Alger Hiss*. Hiss was convicted of being a Communist spy. Jowitt defends Hiss, based on the character of his chief accuser (an argument that has since been refuted). Atticus shows something of his politics by saying that the author has "a childlike faith in the integrity of civil servants" (18), expressing a distrust of the federal government that will be enlarged on as the story continues.

On the positive side, after Jean Louise arrives, on her date with Henry, she remembers that Atticus, who was in the legislature, was never supported by or attacked by the crooked "machine" politicians, and that when he retired from state government, the machine took over. Furthermore, Atticus supports Henry in his plan to run for the legislature against the machine.

Also, Atticus still has his dry sense of humor (about Jean Louise and Hank's night swim), and his love of reading multiple newspapers. The reader's and Jean Louise's first clue that something is awry with Atticus's views is when she finds the repulsive pamphlet that he has been reading, a piece of literature that one can't imagine him tolerating in his house in *To Kill a Mockingbird*.

We are equally shocked when we find out from Aunt Alexandra that Atticus is attending a White Citizens' Council meeting, with the less onerous name of the Maycomb Citizens' Council—in the courthouse, no less, where he had once tried to teach all of Maycomb, by his courageous actions, that there should be equality for all, special privileges for none. When Aunt Alexandra innocently adds that not only is Atticus a member of the council but also on the board of directors, Jean Louise is stunned: "Citizens' Council? In Maycomb? . . . Atticus?"

The racism she hears at the meeting, Atticus listening silently from his seat in the front, makes her literally sick—green with nausea. Afterward she remembers what the former Atticus, with his almost Christlike stance, had meant in her life: "She did not stand alone, but what stood behind her, the most potent moral force in her life, was the love of her father. She never questioned it, never thought about it, never even realized that before she made any decision of importance the reflex, 'What would Atticus do?' passed through her unconscious . . . she did not know that she worshiped him" (117, 118).

Jean Louise is curt and cold to Atticus when she first sees him after the courthouse meeting a day later. But she has some momentary hope that he isn't truly the man she saw at the meeting when she hears him tell Hank that "of course" they will take the case of Zeebo's son and defend him against a charge of killing a drunk man who wandered in front of his car at night.

Then she discovers with horror that the only reason Atticus is taking the case is to keep the NAACP away from town. He calls the organization's black lawyers "buzzards." Alone, she thinks that at one time "Atticus would have done it simply from his goodness, he would have done it for Cal" (150).

She remembers Atticus's manners, so at variance with what she has just seen of his racial philosophy—the man who "would not be discourteous to a ground squirrel" had listened without dissent in that courthouse. She had seen him waiting his turn behind black people in line. She had been taught by Calpurnia and Atticus to treat everyone, no matter how lowly, with respect.

She goes to Uncle Jack for clarification: "What is the matter with Atticus?" and again, later into the senseless conversation, wondering, "what the hell has happened to my father?" (199). Uncle Jack answers her with literary riddles.

She leaves Uncle Jack and goes to find Atticus, only to end up in a cafe with Henry, where she learns that her saintly father had once joined the Ku Klux Klan. Henry defends Atticus's choice by saying that he had been to only one meeting, and had joined to know the enemy. This explanation does not pacify Jean Louise who says cynically, "He's probably the Grand Dragon by now" (230).

In an unpleasant meeting afterward, Atticus's revelations about his opinions enrage Jean Louise and break her heart. She seems to have gone in to try to discover he isn't the man his presence at the Maycomb Citizens' Council has proved him to be.

Instead, he justifies the council. He hates the federal government and the NAACP. He discloses that he, like the man at the meeting, believes black people are a lower form of civilization, incapable of participating in government, and threatening to white culture. And he is a dyed-in-the-wool segregationist. When Jean Louise says she thinks the South deserves every problem the NAACP has dropped on its doorstep, Atticus shockingly replies: "Then let's put this on a practical basis right now. Do you want Negroes by the carload in our schools and churches and theaters? Do you want them in our world?" (245).

Hero, Human, or Villain?

What occurs to Jean Louise at this point could very well be the words of many fans of *To Kill a Mockingbird*. She thinks: "Everything that was Gospel to her she got at home from her father. You sowed the seeds in me, Atticus. . . . . I'll never forgive you for what you did to me. You cheated me" (248).

Uncle Jack's intervention, to persuade her to remain home for the rest of her vacation, is an unsatisfactory end to the novel. It is simply not at all convincing. She seems to have learned from Jack to tolerate Atticus's views, but the extent of the racism he expresses in his office and the extent of the outrage she conveys toward him are too great to be so suddenly overturned by the information that Atticus has a different conscience from hers and that she is being a bigot by not understanding his views.

Nevertheless, the final scene of the book presents a positive take on Atticus. Father and daughter reconcile and he tells her he is proud of her. "Well, I certainly hope a daughter of mine'd hold her ground for what she thinks is right—stand up to me first of all" (277).

The suggested solution is that Atticus, her father, and the reader's idol has now become a human being. This is scarcely a resolution for the reader.

That this Atticus of *Go Set a Watchman* was conceived and written first, *before* the portrait of the Christlike Atticus of *To Kill a Mockingbird*, presents a complication too problematical to try to unravel.

Megan Garber voices the challenge to a longstanding hero in our culture, in which children and businesses have long been named for Atticus, his portrait has inspired people to follow the law as a profession, and he has become "an intimate figure in many lives." She asks, "What are we to do upon learning that the man who was so stubborn in his sense of justice has chosen, in the end, to live on the wrong side of history?"

Two essays present two very different ways of looking at the changes in the character of Atticus: Michiko Kakutani in a *New York Times* review was shocked by the portrait of Atticus as a racist; his "abhorrent views on race and segregation" is "disorienting," and "makes for disturbing reading" "Review"). Alexandra Alter, also of the *New York Times*, presents a very different reading, writing that "after the initial shock of the change in Atticus, we see a more complex but harsh reality of race in the South than we get in a 'sugar coating' of racial divisions in *To Kill a Mockingbird.*"

Further Reading

Interview with Professor Neal Lester, Arizona State University.

Allison, Scott T., and George R. Goethals. *Heroes: What They Do and Why We Need Them.* Richmond: University of Richmond Scholarship Repository, 2011.

Alter, Alexandra . "Racism in *Go Set a Watchman* Could Alter Harper Lee's Legacy." *New York Times,* July 11, 2015. https://www.nytimes.com/2015/07/12/books/racism-of-atticus-finch-in-go-set-a-watchman-could-alter-harper-lees-legacy.html?_r=0.

Cochran, Johnnie. *California Lawyer* (May 2002).

Freedman, Monroe. "Atticus Finch, Esq., R.I.P.: A Gentleman but No Model for Lawyers." *Legal Times*, February 24, 1992, 19–26.

Garber, Megan. "Go Set a Legacy: The Fate of Harper Lee." *The Atlantic*, February 2, 2016. https://www.theatlantic.com/entertainment/archive/2016/02/harper-lee-to-kill-a-mockingbird/470118/.

Harris, Elizabeth A. "Bearing Name of Beloved Father and Lawyer, and Now a Racist." *New York Times*, July 15, 2015, A21.

Kakutani, Michiko. "Kind Hero of 'Mockingbird' Returns as Racist in Sequel." *New York Times*, July 11, 2015, A1.

Kakutani, Michiko. "Review: Harper Lee's 'Go Set a Watchman' Gives Atticus Finch a Dark Side." *New York Times*, July 10, 2015. https://www.nytimes.com/2015/07/11/books/review-harper-lees-go-set-a-watchman-gives-atticus-finch-a-dark-side.html?action=click&contentCollection=Books&module=RelatedCoverage&region=Marginalia&pgtype=article.

King, Martin Luther Jr. *Why We Can't Wait.* New York: Penguin, 1964.

Kovaleski, Serge F., and Alexandra Alter. "A New Account of 'Watchman's Origin and Hints of a Third Book." *New York Times*, July 14, 2015, A16.

Lee, Harper. *Go Set a Watchman.* New York: HarperCollins, 2015.

Lee, Harper. *To Kill a Mockingbird.* Philadelphia: J. B. Lippincott, 1960. Warner Books paperback edition, 1982.

Phelps, Teresa Godwin. "The Margins of Maycomb: A Rereading of *To Kill a Mockingbird.*" *Alabama Law Review* 45, no. 2 (Winter 1994): 511–30.

"Plot Twist: Atticus Finch, Transformed." (Letters to the Editor). *New York Times*, July 14, 2015, A120.

Shaffer, Thomas. "The Moral Theology of Atticus Finch." *University of Pittsburgh Law Review* 42, no. 181 (1981).

Shilling, Jane. "Why I Won't Be Reading *Go Set a Watchman.*" *The Telegraph*, July 12, 2015. http://www.telegraph.co.uk/culture/books/11734978/Why-I-wont-be-reading-Go-Set-a-Watchman.html.

CHAPTER NINE

Impact and Censorship

The influence of *To Kill a Mockingbird* forms one of the more fascinating chapters in American literature. Even 65 years after its publication, it retains its position as an American masterpiece and one of the most frequently read and taught novels in the canon. Its importance is also seen in its impact on the lives of individuals.

Awards and Recognition

The first acknowledgment of the novel's greatness was being chosen for the Pulitzer Prize in the year of its publication. Immediately, as well, filmmakers sought the right to adapt it. The film made from the novel won three Academy Awards. One year after its publication in 1960, it had sold 500,000 copies and had been translated into ten languages.

In a 1970s study of the best-sellers in the 80-year period between 1895 and 1975, *To Kill a Mockingbird* was found to be the seventh best-selling book in the history of American publishing and the third best-selling novel. By 1992, Popular Library and Warner Books had issued 18 million paperback copies alone. Since it was published in 1960, it has never been out of print in either hardcover or paperback.

In repeated surveys by the Library of Congress, it is second only to the Bible in being cited as the book that "most changed my life." Using 5,000 respondents in 1991, the Book of the Month Club and the Library of Congress Center for the Book found that one of the three books "most often cited as making a difference" in people's lives was Harper Lee's *To Kill a Mockingbird*. And in a 1997 survey in England to determine what readers regarded as the greatest books in the English language, *To Kill a Mockingbird* came in sixth. When Random House's editorial board in 1999 left the novel entirely out of its 100 greatest novels of the century, less formal polls were taken to protest the Random House list. One conducted by the *Boston Globe* placed *To Kill a Mockingbird* at the top of the list.

In 1975, 11,113,909 copies of the book had been sold; by 1982 over 15 million; by 2016, over 40 million copies had been sold. As late as 2017, the novel was still selling over one million copies a year and has now been translated into more than 40 languages.

Through the years, *To Kill a Mockingbird* has won numerous awards besides the Pulitzer. In 1961, the year after publication, it won the Brotherhood Award of the National Conference of Christians and Jews and the Alabama Library Association Award. In the next year, it won the Bestsellers Paperback of the Year Award. In 1999, the *Library Journal* presented it with the Best Novel of the Century award.

Continued Worldwide Appeal

During 2016, articles about the release of *Go Set a Watchman* ran with regularity in the English-speaking world's top newspapers, sometimes on the front page, including the *New York Times* and *The Guardian.*

The remarkable fact is that this novel about a tiny village in Alabama in the 1930s has had worldwide appeal. Varinder Singh, even as recently as February 24, 2016, wrote: "One of the most influential novels of the 20th century is without a doubt *To Kill a Mockingbird*, the infamous Pulitzer Prize winning novel that turned literature across the world on its head."

What is so astounding is that from the perspective of 56 years after the publication of the novel and after the controversial release of *Go Set a Watchman*, writers in first-rate journals, like *Vogue* and the *New Yorker*, still praise the legacy of *To Kill a Mockingbird*, not only for its literary excellence but for its influence. Several commentators, looking back, state that it fueled the civil rights movement. Caroline Chavez, writing in *Reverb Press*, states the following: "The novel was certainly a revolutionary one, which is why it is a classic of American literature to this day. . . . Indeed, the impact of *To Kill a Mockingbird* is still present today. . . . today *To Kill a Mockingbird* both in novel form and in the form of film . . . continues moving minds around the world." The title of Nathan Heller's February 2016 article in *Vogue* says it all: "Remembering Harper Lee and the Book That Meant Almost Everything to Everyone."

Censorship

To Kill a Mockingbird is one of the most widely read novels of all time. Ever since its publication in 1960, it has also been one of the books most frequently challenged by would-be censors. Objections have been raised to its presence on library shelves and to its assignment as required reading in schools. To illustrate the enduring pertinence of the novel, in the fall of 1993—some thirty-three years after its publication—two headlined stories in national newspapers addressed issues central to the novel: censorship in the public schools and the stereotyping of African Americans.

A careful look reveals that most of the elements objected to by challengers of novels in general can be found in Harper Lee's first book: (1) references to the sex act, (2) slang and ungrammatical speech, (3) curse words and obscene language, (4) racial slurs, (5) description of rebelliousness and challenges to authority, (6) unfavorable portrayals of the establishment and traditions, (7) the questioning of absolutes, (8) perceived racism and stereotyping. Author Julian Thompson boils the categories down to three: (1) vulgar language, (2) references to sexual activity, and (3) expression of anti-establishment attitudes.

The First Major Challenge to the Novel

The first challenge to *To Kill a Mockingbird* that received notice was mounted in Hanover County, Virginia, in 1966. It got attention because Harper Lee herself became involved in it. The incident began when a prominent physician, W. C. Bosher, the father of a Hanover County student, took a look at the novel his son had brought home to read and decided it was immoral. Dr. Bosher, who was also a County Board of Education trustee, was disturbed that his son was reading a book about rape and reported to the board that the book was "improper for our children to read." On the strength of his motion, the board voted to remove the novel from the shelves of the Hanover County school libraries.

In the flurry of reportage and exchange of opinions that followed, the board blamed the state, arguing that the County Board had had the novel removed because *To Kill a Mockingbird* had never been on the state's list of books approved for state subsidy. When the State Board of Education was challenged about banning the novel, it pointed the finger at the county, saying that the county was free to keep the book on county shelves. It was finally discovered that thousands of books presented by publishers for places on the approved list had been rejected by the state's censoring board. In most cases, except for Dr. Bosher's statements to the press, no reason for rejection by county or state was ever given to the public.

The controversy over *To Kill a Mockingbird* was documented in the pages of the Richmond press: news stories reporting the actions of the board, editorials, letters to the editor on both sides of the question, and a response from the author. Eventually, the board backed away from its original decision to take the book out of the library.

The *Richmond News Leader*, on its editorial page, objected to the board's initial prohibition: "A more moral novel scarcely could be imagined," and, using strong language, suggested a remedy for the board's action: "Fortunately, there exists a remedy for this asinine performance." From its "Beadle Bumble Fund," the paper stated that it would buy a copy of the book for any high school student who wrote in with a request (January 5, 1966, 12).

Other standard works did not appear on the state's approved list and would, therefore, require successful petitions to be on the library shelves. Those included George Orwell's *1984*, John Steinbeck's *Grapes of Wrath*, and J. D. Salinger's *Catcher in the Rye*.

One letter to the editor suggested other books for possible banning: "Regarding the removal of 'To Kill a Mockingbird' from the library shelves of the Hanover school, I suggest the Hanover County School Board check closely into 'Rebecca of Sunnybrook Farm.' Also I thought that several passages in 'Five Little Peppers and How They Grew' were pretty gamey" (*Richmond News Leader*, January 12, 1966, 8). Tons of letters supporting the ban were written to the paper and tons objecting to the board's action came from noted journalists and writers, including one from Harper Lee herself.

Objections to Language and Scout's Character

At the time of *To Kill a Mockingbird*'s appearance and later in the 1960s, the book was objected to chiefly because it included bad language and references to sex, rape, and incest. The main character, Scout, was seen to be a terrible role model for young people, especially little girls. There was much opposition to the exposure of the racist society in the South and the favorable and sympathetic views of black people. So the initial negative response came from white ultra-conservatives on the right and in the South, like the case in Virginia. But by the 1980s, the book was challenged more often by black parents and those on the left for its perceived stereotyping of black characters and for the use of racist slurs.

Kenya Downs in an online article for the *PBS Newshour* summarized some of a selected few of the challenges to *To Kill a Mockingbird* in the public schools, beginning in the late 1970s, many of them coming from the Midwest. In 1977, in Eden Valley, Minnesota, the book was contested because of its use of "damn" and "whore lady." In 1980, in Vernon Verona Sherrill schools in New York, the book was challenged because it was "a filthy, trashy novel." In 1981, in Warren, Indiana, and in 1984 Waukegan, Illinois, school districts protested its "institutional racism" and racist slurs (along with *Huckleberry Finn* and *Gone With the Wind*). In 1985, the novel was challenged in Kansas City and Park Hill, Missouri, for profanity and racial slurs and in the same year, the NAACP and black parents objected to the novel's profanity and racial slurs. In 1995 and 1996, it was banned or challenged for the same reasons in Santa Cruz, California; Caddo Parish, Louisiana; and Moss Point, Mississippi. The novel was banned in Lindale, Texas, because it conflicted with the values of the community. Challenges continued into the 21st century, up through 2017, chiefly on the grounds of profanity and racial slurs—in Georgia, Oklahoma, Illinois, North Carolina, Tennessee, New Jersey, Ontario, Texas, and Arizona. In 2013, a twelve-year ban of the novel was lifted in Plaquemines Parish, Louisiana (Karolides, Bald, and Sova, *100 Banned Books*, 404–6). In October of 2017, it was removed from a school reading list because of complaints about the language.

Self-Censorship Regarding *Go Set a Watchman*

As in other cases, there is the irony that one of the world's most famous, admired, and frequently read novels is also one of the most censored ones. The other irony here on the matter of censorship is that readers who adored *To Kill a Mockingbird* are self-censoring when it comes to *Go Set a Watchman*. Journalists and other avid readers have announced that they will not be reading Harper Lee's last book. As Jane Shilling writes in "Why I Won't Be Reading *Go Set a Watchman*," "The Atticus of *Watchman* is not the righteous authority figure beloved by generations of readers, but an ageing, arthritic racist."

Further Reading

"Censorship and English: Some Things We Don't Seem to Think about Very Often (But Should)." *Focus* 3 (1978): 18–24.

Chavez, Caroline. "Why the Legacy of Harper Lee's *To Kill a Mockingbird* Still Matters." *Reverb Press*, February 19, 2016.

Dave, R. A. "*To Kill a Mockingbird*: Harper Lee's Tragic Vision." In *Indian Studies in American Fiction*, edited by M. K. Naik, S. K. Desai, and S. Mokashi-Punekar, 26–30. Dharwar: Karnatak University and the Macmillan Company of India, 1974.

Downs, Kenya. "*To Kill a Mockingbird* Remains among Top Banned Classical Novels." *PBS Newshour*, February 19, 2016. http://www.pbs.org/newshour /rundown/to-kill-a-mockingbird-remains-among-top-banned-classical -novels/.

Editorial. "Mr. Bumble and the Mockingbird." *Richmond News Leader*, Jan. 5, 1966, 12.

Hefley, James C. *Are Textbooks Harming Your Children?* Milford, MI: Mott Media, 1979.

Heller, Nathan. "Remembering Harper Lee and the Book That Meant Almost Everything to Everyone." *Vogue*, Feb. 19, 2016.

Karolides, Nicholas J., Margaret Bald, and Dawn B. Sova. "*To Kill a Mockingbird*," In *100 Banned Books*, 476–84. New York: Checkmark Books, 1999.

Lee, Harper. "Letter to the Editor." *Richmond News Leader*, January 15, 1966, 10.

May, Jill P. "Censors as Critics: *To Kill a Mockingbird* as a Case Study." In *Cross-Culturalism in Children's Literature*, 1. New York: Pace University, 1989.

May, Jill P. "In Defense of *To Kill a Mockingbird*." In *Censored Books: Critical Viewpoints,* edited by Nicholas J. Karolides, Lee Burress, and John M. Kean, 476–84. Metuchen, NJ: Scarecrow Press, 1993.

"Mississippi School District Pulls 'To Kill a Mockingbird' for Making People 'Uncomfortable.'" *CBS News*, October 16, 2017. https://www.cbsnews .com/news/to-kill-a-mockingbird-book-mississippi-school-district -removes-lesson-plan/.

Shilling, Jane. "Why I Won't Be Reading *Go Set a Watchman*." *The Telegraph*, July 12, 2015. http://www.telegraph.co.uk/culture/books/11734978/Why-I -wont-be-reading-Go-Set-a-Watchman.html.

Singh, Varinder. "The Song of the Mockingbird—The Legacy of Harper Lee." *NUBI*, February 24, 2016.

Thompson, Julian. "Defending YA Literature against the Pharisees and Censors: Is It Worth the Trouble?" *ALAN Review* 18, no. 2 (1991): 2–5.

CHAPTER TEN

Relevance Today of Issues in Harper Lee's Novels

Issues and themes in Harper Lee's two novels still resonate in the 21st century. Matters of racial injustice arise daily in the newspapers, including police shootings of unarmed black men and arguments over gerrymandering that prevent minorities from exercising their full voting rights. Terrorism and hate groups similar to the Ku Klux Klan have risen to the surface in recent years as well. Attempts to purge communities of monuments to Mrs. Dubose's "Old South," have triggered sometimes violent protest.

On the topic of gender, women, seeking to avoid the "coffee party," little-girl kind of life, are finding many more routes to independence and even power, but are meeting impediments as well.

And, finally, of relevance today is the subject of the hero and the problem for society of dealing with the fallen hero, like Atticus.

Police Shootings and Misconduct

Flooding the media in the 2010s are stories of the shooting of unarmed black men by police officers. Concern with this surfaced on August 9, 2014, with the killing of 18-year-old Michael Brown in Ferguson, Missouri. A policeman approached Brown, who was unarmed, on suspicion he had robbed a small grocery market of merchandise. The policeman shot Brown from the window of his car and then followed him, shooting a total of 12 rounds, killing him. Controversy arose over the eyewitness accounts: some said Brown had his arms in the air; some said he began running toward the policeman; some said he was backing away from the officer. Violent protests broke out in the black community, but the officer was never indicted. After an investigation, the United States Justice Department ordered reviews and changes in the police department (Buchanan, "What Happened," 14).

In the same year of 2014, a call was placed to dispatchers in the police department of Cleveland, Ohio, reporting a child playing with what appeared to be a toy gun around a recreational center. A call went out to officers, without mentioning the probability of a fake gun or of the owner's being a child. Officers approached in a car and shot the black 12-year-old dead. Although an administrative investigation was launched, no criminal charges were filed against the three officers involved (Heisig, "Tamir Rice," 1).

Also in 2014, in Chicago, Illinois, officer Jason Van Dyke shot a black teenager 16 times as he was walking away. The defense and the police union argued that the officer felt his life was in danger, and three other fellow officers with decades on the police force corroborated the shooter's story. The video of the shooting that came to light showed their version of the shooting to be false. Van Dyke was arrested the day the video was released. The three other officers who had come to his defense earlier were charged with covering up the circumstances of the shooting to protect Van Dyke. The incident caused massive protests in Chicago and dismissal of the police superintendent. The U.S. Justice Department also began an investigation, finding that the Chicago police force had a pattern of routinely using excessive force and violating the rights of minorities. The investigation's findings forced reforms within the department and an attempt at better relations between police and communities.

Most of the cases that have arisen since Ferguson were reportedly traffic stops, involved unarmed black men, and were videotaped, providing a visual record of just how the killings occurred. In a surprising number of these cases, the officers involved were not charged or were not found guilty in court. Two instances, of many, regarding racial injustice in the killings of black males by policemen received attention in 2016 and 2017.

In St. Anthony, Minnesota, on July 6, 2016, Philando Castile, a black man, was pulled over for a broken tail light and was reaching for his driver's license when he was shot repeatedly from outside the driver's window by an officer, thinking the victim was going for his gun. A woman and her four-year-old daughter were in the car at the time. The officer was acquitted of second-degree manslaughter and all other charges. In this case, as in many others, the family of the victim received settlements from the city, but "Mr. Castile's case is the latest example of a police shooting of a black person leading to a legal settlement but no criminal conviction of the officer involved." President Barack Obama and the governor of Minnesota both asked, "Would this have happened if the driver were white, if the passenger were white?" (Smith, "Officer Cleared," A1).

In September of 2016, a white female police officer shot and killed an unarmed black man whom she was wrongly convinced had a gun. He was walking away from her, back to his car, with his hands up. He had been stopped for a traffic violation and did not appear to be threatening in any way. She was armed with a taser but chose instead to shoot him when, she reported, he began reaching into his car window. Testimony at trial in Tulsa, Oklahoma, in May of 2017, claimed that he could not have reached into the window because it was rolled up. Still the officer testified that she acted in accordance with her training (Walinches, "Tulsa Officer," A17).

Voting Rights

The issue of race and injustice persists to the present day in the matter of voting rights for black people, a topic that arises in *Go Set a Watchman*. Five years after the publication of *To Kill a Mockingbird*, in 1965, the Voting Rights Act was passed by the United States Congress and signed into law by President Lyndon Johnson. Its purpose was to end voting discrimination, specifically to take down barriers to voting on the part of African Americans. It has been called the most effective piece of civil rights legislation ever passed.

Nine states, notorious for impediments to voting, were targeted for oversight by the Justice Department, which could monitor voter registration and voting sites in states like Alabama. Sections 2 and 5 were most important. They targeted gerrymandering, designed to redraw districts to curtail black voting, and voting laws, like tests and other devices, that had the intention of making voting on the part of black people difficult. (Jean Louise, on her way home in *Go Set a Watchman*, describes Maycomb County as "a gerrymander some seventy miles long" [7].) For instance, the Voting Rights Act outlawed literacy tests and required certain states and districts to seek federal approval for any changes in voting requirements.

In 2010, states began speeding up the passage of new restrictive voting laws, resulting in impediments to the voting of minorities, the poor, students, and the elderly. These impediments included new ID requirements, restrictions on early voting, and cutting back the time to register and to vote. By 2012 19 states had passed 25 restrictive voting laws, some of which were struck down in courts of appeals. In North Carolina, the court called the new laws "the most restrictive voting laws North Carolina has seen since the era of Jim Crow." Texas attempted to reinstate old voting laws including the redrawing of district maps, which were found to be discriminatory. Alabama and Mississippi did the same thing. Evergreen, Alabama, for example, a town mentioned in *Go Set a Watchman*, was 62 percent African American, but had a majority of whites on the city council.

In a case in 2013, the Supreme Court, in *Shelby County v. Holder*, gutted the core of the Voting Rights Act, ruling that states were freed from oversight because voting restrictions were no longer a threat. In essence, this turned key decisions back to the states. Still the controversy went on.

Racial gerrymandering was challenged by the Alabama Legislative Caucus and the Alabama Democratic Conference. In 2015, a federal appeals court ruled that twelve districts in Alabama had turned to gerrymandering to shrink the black vote and keep a Republican majority. African Americans had been packed into oddly shaped areas to limit their influence. The court called on the state to have a nonpartisan commission to redraw voting maps before the 2020 election. When the appeals case reached the Supreme Court, it was sent back to the lower court whose decision then was confirmed (Rutenberg, "Dream Undone"; Liptak, "Supreme Court"; Ollstein, "Alabama Found Guilty").

Other states also began enacting racial discriminatory voting practices. North Carolina, for example, passed legislation rejecting forms of identification most easily available to black people. These included government employee IDs, student IDs, and IDs of people on public assistance. The new laws cut same-day registration and preregistration for some, and banned counting of votes in the wrong precinct. Although there was no evidence of voting fraud, this was the rationalization given for more stringent qualifications for voting, all disproportionately affecting African American voting.

The fight over voting affected by the drawing of districts continues in Alabama. In May of 2017, a Republican plan of redistricting submitted to the legislature was rejected by Democrats who said that "the new map is still gerrymandered to maintain white GOP dominance," and to minimize black voters. One white Republican engaged in the fight sent out an email: "ALL of the monkeys need to be REPLACED" (Chandler, "Alabama Democrats," A3).

As in the Alabama case, an appeals court struck down the North Carolina state voting laws, and in May of 2017, the Supreme Court refused to hear the case, leaving the appeals court decision in place. The American Civil Liberties Union praised the decision as closing an "ugly chapter in voter suppression," but the North Carolina legislature vowed to implement the new restrictions again (Liptak with Wines, "Justices Thwart," A1). In another article, journalist Adam Liptak writes: "The Supreme Court struck down two North Carolina Congressional Districts on Monday [May 22], ruling that lawmakers had violated the Constitution by relying too heavily on race in drawing them." This was the second decision against North Carolina, which was deemed one of the worst offenders (Liptak, "Justices Reject," A19).

The Simultaneous Return and Fall of the Old South

In the second decade of the 21st century, more than 150 years after the Civil War was fought, a bizarre series of actions and reactions occurred, having to do with racism and the symbols of Mrs. Dubose's Old South. These events seemed to have been triggered by the rise of a movement called the alternative right, or "alt right." This is a white nationalist (supremacist) movement supporting white identity and Western civilization against what its adherents see as their enemies, including blacks, Jews, and immigrants. The most extreme of them, of which there are more than a few, believe that ideally black people should be returned to Africa and Jews to Israel. They reject equality and universalism ("Alternative Right"). Even the conservative Southern Baptists, after a lively discussion, voted to condemn the alt right. The resolution was "to reject the retrograde ideologies, xenophobic biases, and racial bigotries of the 'Alt Right'" (Bailey, "Southern Baptists," 2).

The racism of such ideology expressed itself in violence on June 17, 2015, in Charleston, South Carolina, when a young man named Dylann Roof entered a prayer meeting in Charleston's downtown Emanuel African Methodist Episcopal Church. Roof had that day, and in the days before, made a point of visiting sites with an Old South history, including plantations and other places connected to slavery. On Sullivan's Island, just outside Charleston, where slaves were brought into the antebellum South, he drew meaningful numbers in the sand—"1488" standing for a racist creed to secure the future for white children, and "88," standing for HH or Heil Hitler. Roof took numerous pictures of himself with a Confederate flag and one of himself with a burning American flag. He also wrote documents about his admiration for Germans and Nazism in particular, and kept up with a registered white supremacist website.

A little after 8:30 p.m., he entered the prayer meeting, where he was welcomed and handed religious literature. After nearly an hour, he rose with his Glock .45-caliber pistol and began firing. As he stood and began firing he accused the church members of raping white women and taking over the world, and then reloaded, firing 77 rounds, eventually killing nine people. His jailhouse writings, railing against black and Jewish people, were admitted into evidence. He was accused and found guilty of 33 crimes, including violation of the Hate Crimes Act and obstruction of the exercise of religion (Ball, "United States v. Dylann Roof," 1).

In the 1940s, the Confederate flag's importance had revived as a symbol of segregation. And into the 1950s it was taken up by the Dixiecrats who objected to President Harry Truman's antidiscrimination law and antilynching legislation. In 1963, Governor George Wallace of Alabama and leaders in other Southern states raised the flag to protest racial integration. The Confederate flag was again flown by the Ku Klux Klan in the mid 1950s (Hanson, "Confederate Flag").

The reaction to the Charleston killings in many Southern states and immediately in South Carolina, was to take down the symbol of the Old South—the Confederate flag—in which Dylann Roof had wrapped himself and which waved over many Southern state houses. Some people argued that it was a racially neutral symbol of Southern culture, but others, who objected to it, saw (as killer Roof did) a racist symbol of a region that seceded from the United States in an attempt to maintain slavery. Confederate flags were removed from license plates, public parks, and military cemeteries. Walmart, Sears, K-Mart, Target, and other stores removed the flag from ads and merchandise (Hanson, "Confederate Flag"). (In fact, however, the Confederate flag remains as part of state flags in Alabama, Arkansas, Florida, Mississippi, and Georgia.)

Within two years of the Charleston massacre, states and cities began to also take down Confederate monuments, notably statues of Confederate generals—monuments that held up racists as heroes. In New Orleans in 2017 four such monuments were removed from government and public properties, sometimes in the dead of night. These included an obelisk commemorating a Civil War battle and white supremacy, and three statues of Confederate generals. The last to go was one of Robert E. Lee in Lee Circle. (One remembers Robert E. Lee Ewell.) The event, the result of a 2015 city council decision, was greeted with both ill feeling and rejoicing. Some mourned the decision to banish what they saw as valuable Southern history, remembering the Civil War. Protests against taking down memorials included people carrying the Confederate flag (Fausset, "Tempers Flare," A16). Others rejoiced over the demolition of symbols of a pseudo-romantic class- and race-driven society. A black woman, whose ancestor was stolen at eleven years old from his mother and sold as a slave, made a point of attending the taking down of the Robert E. Lee statue in New Orleans: "I thought: 'It's about time. It's about time.' You know, he was standing there with his arms folded as if he was surveying all that was his" (Robertson and Reckdah, "Stories," A13).

The title of a *New York Times* editorial sums up the next phase in the battle against the old racist South: "As Statues Fall, the Specter of the Noose Rises." The symbol of lynchings, white supremacy, intimidation, and terror aimed at black people has been, since the early days of Reconstruction (reminiscent of the Old Sarum mob threatening Atticus in front of the jail), the noose, used by white terrorists to take the lives of black people. Nooses have been left in the yards of black people, in schoolyards, even at businesses in 2017. In the weekend of May 20, 2017, a Mississippi state representative put on Facebook his belief that the people who had arranged for the removal of Confederate statues in New Orleans should be lynched.

In spring of 2017, three nooses at separate times were left at the new National Museum of African American History and Culture in Washington, DC. Lonnie G. Bunch III, director of the museum, writes of the nooses: "[D]iscrimination is not confined to the past." He speaks of nooses also being left as warnings in a Missouri high school and on the campus of Duke University (Bunch, "Noose," A25). A noose was discovered in a tree near the Hirshhorn Museum on the Washington, DC, National Mall, at American University, and at a Washington elementary school (Stolberg and Dickerson, "Nooses," A11). Terrorists with nooses are not confined to the American South in 2017. On May 26, 2017, numerous nooses were found throughout a terminal at the Port of Oakland in California. The incidents prompted a walk-out on the part of workers (Harris and Fraley, "Nooses," B1).

In summer and fall of 2017, the romance of Mrs. Dubose's Confederacy and the presence of the monuments to the Old South they represented exploded on the national scene. As many historians, including Eric Foner, clarified, these statues were created long after the Civil War, after Reconstruction, some as late as the civil rights era of the 1950s and 1960s, to enshrine the idea of racial segregation and white supremacy at a time when the Ku Klux Klan was at its peak ("Confederate Statues," A23). They were built to honor Confederate generals who fought to maintain a brutal slave-holding society.

An explosive episode began on the night of August 11 in Charlottesville, Virginia, when a group of armed militants mobbed the University of Virginia campus to protest the moving of a monument of Robert E. Lee. These were avowed white supremacists, screaming anti-Jewish and racist rants, carrying both Confederate and Nazi flags and banners and presenting

Nazi salutes. When they returned to the town streets on Saturday the 12th, they were confronted by counter-protestors against white supremacy, many of them ministers. At one point, a young avowed Nazi plowed a car into a crowd of counter-protestors, killing a woman and injuring 34 other people.

This violent occurrence resulted in the accelerated relocating of monuments by state governments and was covered by the press daily as the most turbulent national story in a year of continual turbulence.

The Independent Woman

Jean Louise in *Go Set a Watchman* is seeking independence and her own self-identity in the 1950s. She is concerned about the loss of independence she would suffer in marriage, specifically to Henry, and the loss of selfhood she would face in her Southern home town. To marry and live in Maycomb would be to remain a subservient child. The narrator's many views of marriage in the novel are negative. There is not one marriage, prospect of marriage, or theory of marriage that is positive. The "girls" at the coffee party speak of their children as if they are dolls. The woman to whose conversation she gives most attention is intellectually a slave to her husband. Jean Louise's views of the typical Birmingham marriage and New York marriage are entirely negative. For that matter, there are no portraits of happy marriages in *To Kill a Mockingbird* either.

In the eyes of society, the proper vocation of any female is still being a wife and mother, even if one's talents and inclinations do not fit her for marriage and motherhood. And, Kristine M. Baber and Katherine R. Allen write, patriarchal, traditional families are "tension-filled arenas, loci of struggle and domination between genders and across generations" (*Women and Families*, 1). Women are taught to put the needs of those they care for so far above their own needs (for education, training, and career, for example), that it leads to frustration and deprivation.

By 2014, the Pew Research Center found that the percentage of people who had never married had reached an all-time peak of 17 percent. In the United States in the late 2010s the marriage rate is still about 80 percent of the population but fewer people marry and many more people marry much later in life than the women of the 1950s. The number of people whose priorities are other than marriage has also risen and the divorce rate continually rises (Wang and Parker, "Record Share," 1–4).

The culture's views of women, still in the 2010s, undermine their independence, and gender stereotypes persist. Boys who try to lead are admired and called smart. Girls who try to lead are called bossy. Girls are mostly praised with the adjective pretty whereas boys are praised with being strong. Studies have shown that teachers pay more attention to boys than girls in the classroom. Sheryl Sandberg writes that this attitude persists even with female CEOs like herself. At high-level meetings, men are allowed to interrupt a speaker but women are told "let me finish" (Sandberg, *Lean In*, 18–22). This mind-set was on view for all the world to see in the United States Congress in the spring of 2017 when Elizabeth Warren and Kamala Harris were silenced at congressional hearings.

However, perhaps as a result of the active "second wave" of the women's rights movement, that is seen to have begun with the publication in 1963 of Betty Friedan's *The Feminine Mystique*, there have been positive changes for some married women. More husbands and wives view themselves as partners instead of masters and servants. Many men now take a more active role in housekeeping and childcare and, at the same time, share economic decisions with their wives. But there is still little awareness that full-time housekeepers and child-caring wives should receive reimbursement for their labor (Baber and Allen, *Women and Families*).

Broader concepts of women's roles, more access to higher education, and economic need have all contributed to changes in middle-class households, as women were either forced to or desired to enter the workforce. There is a downside to this situation in that in many households the working woman is now burdened with the second shift taking care of the emotional health of the family, the household chores, and the main responsibility for infants and children, also in addition to her financial contributions (Gerstel and Gross, *Families and Work*).

More attention on the part of women's rights activists has been focused on workplace reforms in recent years. The positive result is sometimes that women who work can have the control and self-esteem that they would not have otherwise. In 2017 there were 104 female House of Representative members and 21 female senators. Over 36.9 percent of lawyers are women and almost half of the physicians in the United States are now women. More and more women are entering these top positions in government, medicine, law, business, and engineering, but they are still underrepresented in high-status positions and over-represented in low-paying professions such as teaching, nursing, and secretarial work.

Still women faced (and face) barriers in the workplace and educational institutions. There is discrimination in hiring, promotions, and pay. At times, women who became pregnant were dismissed; women who had children were not hired; and there was no consideration of the need for family leave. Moreover, sexual harassment on the job continues to be a problem.

Various pieces of legislation have made the working woman's position fairer. A few of the most important are mentioned here. The Civil Rights Act of 1964 forbids discrimination on the basis of sex. In 1972, a law was passed prohibiting discrimination in educational institutions that receive federal aid. In 1986, the Supreme Court made sexual harassment on the job illegal. In 2009, the Lilly Ledbetter Fair Pay Act allows victims of pay discrimination to file complaints with the federal government.

The second and third "waves" of feminism had successfully addressed discrimination in the home and workplace. The "fourth wave," distinguished by the use of online messaging, embraced other civil rights movements and encouraged active involvement in politics (Rand, "The Third Wave").

Women's Empowerment in Pop Culture

In 2017, two years after the publication of *Go Set a Watchman*, an artistic representation of a strong, independent woman, who inspired many girls and had appeared on the cover of *Ms.* magazine in 1972, became the heroine of one of the highest-grossing movies of the year. "Wonder Woman" in the new film is synonymous with power. She is the opposite of the weak, childlike women of the coffee party. She grows up in a powerful female culture without any sense of traditional gender roles. From her childhood, she is trained to obliterate the god of war. Ironically, to do this, she has to be trained as a warrior herself. She is shocked by her first encounter with a pre–World War I society that oppresses women. Women don't even have the right to vote. Because of her background and independence, she is able to view corsets and other symbols of misogyny with a certain amount of ridicule (Scanlan, "Super Role Model").

Some critics have declared it to be the best-reviewed superhero film of all time. Its opening weekend grossed over $100 million in the United States alone, over $200 million worldwide. Although some feminists found Wonder Woman's revealing costumes and nude scenes a reinforcement of the old idea of woman as a sex object, most saw it as a statement of woman's power: she saves her male cohorts; she is defined by her athletic ability; and she battles a large group of soldiers and wins (Lawler, "Spoilers"; Rosenberg, "Thinking"; Williams, "Wonder Woman").

The Honor and Ordeal of Heroism

Heroism brings with it glory and admiration. We see this in *To Kill a Mockingbird* with Atticus, one of the loftiest role models in literature. At the same time, his heroism came with a price in the novel, as townspeople disparage him and his children are placed in danger—his son Jem badly injured.

The same double results affected the greatest hero of 2009, Captain Chesley (Sully) Sullenberger, who held responsibility, as pilot, for the lives of 155 people when his airplane's engines died in the air. He was widely honored for his heroism but also faced questions about his difficult decision.

On January 15, 2009, Sully and his copilot, Jeff Skiles, took off from La Guardia airport in New York for Charlotte, North Carolina. Just after they were cleared for take-off, as they were climbing to their flying altitude (they were only at 3,000 feet), a sizeable flock of Canada geese hit the plane, each bird with a probable weight of 12 pounds. Sully writes of the impact: "The birds struck many places on the aircraft below the level of the windshield, including the nose, wings, and engines. The thuds came in rapid succession, almost simultaneously but a fraction of a fraction of a second apart" (Sullenberger, *Highest Duty*, 207). He knew right away that they had bad engine trouble as a result: "I felt, heard, and smelled evidence that birds had entered the engines—both engines—and severely damaged them. I heard the noise of the engines chewing themselves up inside, as the rapidly spinning, finely balanced machinery was being ruined, with broken blades coming loose" (208, 209).

Sully had only three and a half minutes to make a decision. As he and Skiles tried to make contact with air traffic control and figure out the checklist for dead engines, he turned the plane into a glider and switched on the auxiliary power unit.

Their expected options were to try to return to La Guardia and land or to land in Teterboro, New Jersey. Even Newark was offered as an option. Not only did Sully see the real chance that they wouldn't get to La Guardia, but the danger that the plane, descending so rapidly, would crash into buildings on the way. An airport was simply not an option.

Landing in the Hudson River was risky. Still, there seemed to be no other choice in Sully's judgment as the plane dropped lower and lower, at a greater rate than a normal landing. It took constant, complicated maneuvering to land the plane *on* the water (Sullenberger, *Highest Duty*,).

Finally the plane was floating on the water, but the tail end was rapidly taking on water as the evacuation began. First responders arrived within four minutes and all passengers and crew were saved. Ninety-five people suffered minor injuries and five had more serious injuries, including hypothermia.

Sully was celebrated as a hero, honored by the mayor of New York City, Michael Bloomberg; the United States Air Force Academy; the San

Francisco Giants; the National Football League; and by President Barack Obama. The landing was labeled "the Miracle on the Hudson."

But also, immediately, as so often happens with heroes, there were misgivings and skepticism. Questions arose about his judgment not to try to return to La Guardia. Some members of the National Transportation Safety Board investigated. It was even reported publicly on *CBS News* that Sully could have made it back to La Guardia. And soon an elaborate series of computer simulations began to determine whether the plane could have made it to either Teterboro or La Guardia. The conclusion was that such attempted landings could have ended in crashes. The board determined that Sully had made the right decision (Otterman and Wald, "F.A.A.").

Finally, nothing could really diminish Sully's stature as a hero. His autobiography became a *New York Times* best seller and his fame continues in his retirement.

The Fallen Father/Hero

The Atticus Finch of *To Kill a Mockingbird*, an iconic, courageous, moral figure who inspired so many readers and movie-goers, is a fallen hero in *Go Set a Watchman* because of his unmistakable racism, revealed in his high position in the Maycomb Citizens' Council and the ideas he expressed about segregation and black culture in his long confrontation with Jean Louise toward the end of *Go Set a Watchman*.

A sad and extremely relevant case of the fallen father in real life is in the process of playing out as this book goes to press in 2018. This is the case of 88-year-old Bill Cosby—comedian, author, actor, art collector, commentator, and role model, especially as a father figure, for both whites and blacks.

After a stint in the navy and undergraduate education, he successfully entered the world of acting with the espionage series, *I Spy*, the first time an African American appeared in a starring role in a weekly television series. He received three Emmys for Outstanding Lead Actor in a Drama Series.

Cosby left acting for a while to continue his education, receiving his MA and EdD in education at the University of Massachusetts. He also taught reading skills to children on a PBS series. The role for which he was best known followed in September of 1984 when he started the family-based series, *The Cosby Show*, which constantly received top television ratings until it ended, after a long run, in 1992. It was his role on this show that gave whites and blacks a model for family—parental—relationships. In the press he was awarded the title "American Dad."

Cosby seemed to devote his life to children, education, and to fostering wise and compassionate parenting. The books he authored reflect his interests: among the twelve are *Fatherhood*, *Childhood*, and *American Schools*. One of Cosby's *New York Times* best-selling books, written with Alvin F. Poussaint, *Come On, People*, is directed at the morals of black people. It includes extensive information on sex, praising abstinence. One section in chapter one is entitled "Get Smart About Sex."

His awards over the years are overwhelming in number: in 1998 he received the Kennedy Center Honor; in 2002 the Medal of Freedom and was included in a biographical dictionary of the 100 greatest African Americans compiled by Molefi Kete Asante; in 2005 he was voted by comedians as among the top 50 comic actors; and in 2009 he received the Mark Twain Prize for Humor. He has received 10 Grammy awards and 57 honorary degrees from schools like Brown, Amherst, the University of Pennsylvania, and UCLA (http://www.biography.com/people/bill-cosby-9258468).

Bill Cosby's position as American father began falling apart in the public mind in October of 2014 when charges that he drugged and sexually assaulted a number of women began to be made public. There had been a civil lawsuit as early as 2005 but it was sealed and few people were aware of it. Suddenly many claims of assaults running from 1965 until 2008 came to the surface, with between 40 and 60 women going public. The statute of limitations had passed on many of the cases, but a number of civil suits were filed and more were announced to be forthcoming. One criminal complaint was able to be filed, however, and on December 30, 2015, he was charged in Philadelphia with sexual assault and a warrant was issued for his arrest for drugging and assaulting a woman. Many of his awards and honorary degrees were rescinded.

On Saturday, June 17, in Pittsburgh, the criminal case ended in a mistrial. Prosecutors have said they will try him again.

A May 26, 2017, headline in the *Boston Globe* changed Cosby's old name to "America's Abusive Father." Eugene Robinson, writing for the *Washington Post* on June 21, 2017, sums up Cosby's career: "Cosby's greatness came in the way people could look at him and, in his reflection, see themselves and the nation in a better light. That power is forever gone" (Robinson, "Cosby," A9).

Conclusion

This chapter would suggest that the issues raised in Harper Lee's two novels are not just limited to the 1930s and the beginning of the civil rights era, but are, unfortunately, universal and continuing in nature, presenting constant challenges.

Further Reading

"Alternative Right." Southern Poverty Law Center. www.splcenter.org.

"As Statues Fall the Specter of the Noose Rises." Editorial. *New York Times*, May 25, 2017, A26.

Baber, Kristine M., and Katherine R. Allen. *Women and Families*. New York: Guilford Press, 1992.

Bailey, Sarah Pulliam. "Southern Baptists Voted Overwhelmingly to Condemn Alt-Right Supremacy." *Washington Post*, June 14, 2017, A2.

Ball, Edward. "United States v. Dylann Roof." *New York Review of Books*, March 9, 2017, 1.

Buchanan, Larry. "What Happened in Ferguson." *New York Times*, August 10, 2015, A23.

Bunch, Lonnie G. III. "A Noose Brings History to Life." *New York Times*, June 23, 2017, A25.

Cepeda, Esther. "Skip 'Wonder Woman' and Take Time to Reflect." *Washington Post*, rpt. in *Bay Area News Group*, June 15, 2017, A7.

Chandler, Kim. "Alabama Democrats Vow to Fight Redistricting Plan." Associated Press, in *Bay Area News Group*, May 20, 2017, A3.

Collins, Gail. "Women Move, World Improves." *New York Times*, July 6, 2017, A19.

Cosby, Bill. *Fatherhood*. New York: Berkley Books, 1986.

Cosby, Bill, and Alvin F. Poussaint. *Come On, People*. Nashville: Thomas Nelson, 2007.

Dyson, Michael Eric. *Is Bill Cosby Right? (Or Has the Black Middle Class Lost Its Mind?)*. New York: Perseus Books, 2005.

Fausset, Richard. "Tempers Flare Over Removal of Confederate Statues in New Orleans." *New York Times*, May 7, 2017, A13.

Foner, Eric. "Confederate Statues and 'Our' History." *New York Times*, August 21, 2017, A23.

Friedan, Betty. *The Feminine Mystique*. New York: W. W. Norton, 1997.

Gerstel, Naomi, and Harriet Gross, eds. *Families and Work*. Philadelphia: Temple University Press, 1987.

Hanson, Hilary. "Why the Confederate Flag Is Even More Racist Than You Think." *Huffington Post*, June 22, 2015.

Harris, Harry, and Malaika Fraley. "Nooses Spur Walkout." *Bay Area News Group*, May 26, 2017, B1.

Heilman, Madeline E., and Tyler G. Okimoto. "Why Are Women Penalized for Success at Male Tasks?" *Journal of Applied Psychology* 92, no. 1 (2007): 81–92.

Heisig, Eric. "Tamir Rice Shooting." www.cleveland.com, January 13, 2017.

Kimmel, Michael S., and Amy Aronson, eds. *The Gendered Society Reader*. 3rd ed. Oxford: Oxford University Press, 2008.

Lamont, Marc, and Todd Brewster. *Nobody: Casualties of America's War on the Vulnerable*. New York: Simon and Schuster, 2016.

Langley, Travis. *Wonder Woman Psychology: Lassoing the Truth*. New York: Sterling, 2017.

Langerwiesche, William. "Analogy of a Miracle." *Vanity Fair*, June 2009. www .vanityfair.com.

Lawler, Kelly. "Spoilers: Five Wonderfully Feminist Moments in 'Wonder Woman.'" *USA Today*, June 2, 2017. https://www.usatoday.com/story/life /entertainthis/2017/06/02/5-wonderfully-feminist-moments-wonder -woman-spoilers/102392860/#.

Lepore, Jill. *The Secret History of Wonder Woman*. New York: Random House, 2014.

Liptak, Adam. "Supreme Court Rules Against Alabama in Redistricting Case." *New York Times*, March 25, 2015. www.nytimes.com/2015/03/26/us /supreme-court-rules-against-alabama-in-redistricting-case.html.

Liptak, Adam. "Justices Reject 2 Districts in North Carolina, Citing Packing of Black Voters." *New York Times*, May 22, 2017, A19.

Liptak, Adam, with Michael Wines. "Justices Thwart Strict Voter ID Laws That Unevenly Hurt Blacks." *New York Times*, May 16, 2017, A1.

Marshall, Gloria J. Browne. *The Voting Rights War: The NAACP and the Ongoing Struggle for Justice*. Lanham, MD: Rowman and Littlefield, 2016.

McCann, Anthony J., and Charles Anthony Smith. *Gerrymandering in America*. Cambridge: Cambridge University Press, 2016.

McConnaughey, Janet, and Rebecca Santana. "General Lee Has Left the Obelisk." *Associated Press* in *Bay Area News Group*, May 20, 2017, AA3.

Morris, Wesley. "Two Kinds of Cosby Shows." *New York Times*, June 19, 2017, C1.

Morris, Wesley, and Jenna Wortham. "What Was on Trial in the Cosby Case." *New York Times*, June 25, 2017, Arts 1, 16.

"NTSB: Sully Could Have Made It Back to La Guardia." *CBS News*, May 4, 2010. http://www.cbsnews.com/news/ntsb-sully-could-have-made-it-back -to-laguardia/.

Ollstein, Alice Miranda. "Alabama Found Guilty of Racial Gerrymandering." ThinkProgress, January 20, 2017. www.thinkprogress.org/alabama -found-guilty-of-racial-gerrymanderinge-42148e19c40.

Otterman, Sharon, and Matthew Wald. "F.A.A. Releases Flight 1549 Tapes." *New York Times*, February 5, 2009. A1.

Pasztor, Andy. "'Hudson Miracle' Gets a Closer Look." *Wall Street Journal*, May 4, 2010. https://www.wsj.com/articles/SB10001424052748703612804575222482042335978.

Peques. Jeff. *Black and Blue: Inside the Divide between Police and Black America*. Amherst, MA: Prometheus Books, 2017.

"A Protest with Echoes of the Klan." Editorial. *New York Times*, May 17, 2017, A24.

Rand, Jennifer. "The Third Wave of Feminism Is Now." *Huffington Post*, January 4, 2017. http://www.huffingtonpost.com/entry/the-third-wave-of-femi nism-is-now-and-it-is-intersectional_us_586ac501e4b04d7df167d6a8.

Robertson, Campbell, and Katy Reckdah. "Stories of New Orleans." *New York Times*, May 25, 2017, A13.

Robinson, Eugene. "Cosby and the Crumbling of a True Pop Culture Icon." *Washington Post*, June 21, 2017, A9.

Rosenberg, Alyssa. "When Thinking Goes Outside the Stereotype." *Washington Post*, rpt. in *Bay Area News Group*, June 15, 2017, N4.

Rutenberg, Jim. "A Dream Undone." *New York Times*, July 29, 2015.

Sandberg, Sheryl, with Nell Scovell. *Lean In: Women, Work, and the Will to Lead.* New York: Alfred A. Knopf, 2015.

Saul, Stephanie. "Edging Out of a Confederate Shadow, Gingerly." *New York Times*, August 10, 2017, A10.

Scanlan, Laura Wolfe. "Super Role Model." *Humanities* 34, no. 4 (July/August 2012). https://neh.gov/humanities/2013/julyaugust/statement/super-role.

Seabrook, Nicholas R. *Drawing the Lines: Constraints on Partisan. Gerrymandering in U.S. Politics.* Ithaca, NY: Cornell University Press, 2017.

Smith, Mitch. "Officer Cleared after He Killed a Black Driver." *New York Times*, June 17, 2017, A1.

Stolberg, Sheryl Gay, and Caitlin Dickerson. "Nooses, Protest Symbols of Hate, Crop Up in Rash of Cases." *New York Times*, July 16, 2017, A11.

Stolberg, Sheryl Gay, and Brian M. Rosenthal. "White Nationalist Protest Leads to Deadly Violence." *New York Times*, August 13, 2017, A1.

Sullenberger, Chesley, and Jeffrey Zaslow. *Highest Duty: My Search for What Really Matters.* New York: William Morrow, 2009.

Traister, Rebecca. *All the Single Ladies.* New York: Simon and Schuster, 2016.

Verhaegh, Marcus. *Investigating the Alt-Right.* CreateSpace, 2017.

Walinches, Lucia. "Tulsa Officer Cites Her Training in Testimony About Fatal Shooting of Unarmed Man." *New York Times*, May 16, 2017, A17.

Wang, Wendy, and Kim Parker. "Record Share of Americans Have Never Married." *Pew Research Center*, September 24, 2014, 1–11. www.pewsocial trends.org.

Williams, Michael Paul. "It's Time for Confederate Monuments to Come Down." *Richmond Times-Dispatch*, June 25, 2015.

Williams, Zoe. "Why Wonder Woman Is a Masterpiece of Subversive Feminism." *The Guardian*, June 5, 2017. https://www.theguardian.com/lifeand style/2017/jun/05/why-wonder-woman-is-a-masterpiece-of-subversive -feminism.

Chronology

1880
Lee's father, Amasa Coleman Lee, is born in rural Alabama on July 19.

1909
The NAACP is formed.

1910
Amasa Lee and Frances Finch marry.

1913
The couple moves to Monroeville, Alabama.

1915
Amasa Lee is admitted to the Alabama bar and opens a practice in Monroeville.

1919
He defends two black clients one of whom is executed and one of whom is mutilated.

1924
Truman Capote is born.

1926
Nelle Harper Lee, the youngest of four children, is born to Amasa and Frances Finch Lee on April 28.

1927–1939
Amasa Lee serves as an Alabama state legislator.

1928
When Capote is four years old, his mother begins to leave him for long periods of time with her relatives, who live next door to the Lees.

1929–1947
Amasa edits the *Monroe Journal*.

1931

When Nelle is five, her friendship with Truman Capote begins. They will remain companions as children and into adulthood, as she follows him to New York, appears as a character in his fictions, bases a main character on him in her own first fiction, and becomes essential to his later project *In Cold Blood*.

The notorious Scottsboro Boys trials, in which nine black men are accused of raping two white women, begin in northern Alabama. The trials, appeals, retrials, and pardons go on for 20 years.

1932

U.S. Supreme Court reverses one of the Scottsboro convictions and orders a new trial.

1933

Judge James E. Horton, who was overseeing the trial of one of the Scottsboro defendants, rejects a finding of guilty and subsequently fails to be reelected.

Near Monroeville a black man is arrested on the charge of rape by a poor white woman. Despite objections on the part of much of the Monroeville community and several stays of execution, Walter Lett has a severe mental breakdown and dies four years later in a hospital for the insane.

1934

A mob of KKK members gathers to march to the Monroeville Courthouse and supposedly has a confrontation with Amasa Lee.

1937

All major Alabama newspapers urge the release of the Scottsboro defendants.

1939

The NAACP, founded in 1909, becomes more active and establishes their Legal Defense Fund.

The Daughters of the American Revolution bar famous singer Marian Anderson from performing in Constitution Hall because she is black. Secretary of the Interior Harold Ickes arranges for the concert to move to the steps of the Lincoln Memorial.

1944

Nelle graduates from Monroeville high school and attends Huntingdon College for Women for a year. Except for her writing for campus publications, this is not a positive experience.

1945

In the fall Nelle enrolls at the University of Alabama. Neither her social nor her academic life is satisfying. She moves out of the sorority house after a year and, although she is a writer (editor of the satiric magazine *Rammer Jammer*), the writing program in the English Department does not welcome her nor does she respect it, according to her friend James McMillan.

Her friends from her time at the university are very few and very close: notably, Dr. James McMillan of the English Department and founding director of the University of Alabama Press; John Luskin, a professor of journalism; Ruth Zellner, an editor at the press, married to artist Dick Zellner; and Bill and Doris Leapard.

1946
For the October issue of the *Rammer Jammer*, she writes a one-act play satirizing a Southern politician who called sinful all who wanted to tear down barriers between blacks and whites, and who wants to severely limit the right of blacks to vote. (Alabama had rigid limits at the time on voting for blacks—as it does as of this writing.)

1947
In the February issue she makes fun of country newspapers. One, which had a logo of Klansman burning crosses, was dubbed the *Jackassonian Democrat*.

Nelle enrolls at the University of Alabama Law School, which she attends sporadically. Her impetus is her father's hope that she will follow in his footsteps and those of her older sister Alice. Her own explanation of her motivation for enrolling in law school is so she would be allowed library stack privileges. Her negative views of the law school appear in *Go Set a Watchman*.

1948
Nelle attends Oxford University.

Capote publishes his first major work, *Other Voices, Other Rooms*. One of the characters, the tomboy Idabel, is based, in part, on Nelle Harper.

1949
Nelle finally drops out of law school and moves to New York City, which will be her home until she suffers a paralyzing stroke in 2007. In New York, Nelle supports herself with a job as an airlines reservation clerk for Eastern Air Lines and British Overseas Airways Corporation. She and Truman Capote, who move in different circles in New York, have little to do with one another. Meantime, she continues to write throughout the 1950s on *Go Set a Watchman*.

The last of the Scottsboro defendants is paroled.

1951
After a life with both physical and emotional problems, Nelle's mother dies on June 2.

Nelle's brother, Edwin, also dies of a cerebral hemorrhage a few months later at Maxwell Airfield.

1952
For the first time in 71 years, no lynching is reported during the year. Birmingham is nicknamed "Bombingham."

1954

Public school segregation is ruled unconstitutional by the U.S. Supreme Court in *Brown v. Board of Education*. Mississippi abolishes public schools and sets up private academies in defiance of integration. Twenty-three black children in Montgomery, Alabama, are barred from an all-white public school. The District of Columbia and Maryland end segregation in schools. Protest on the part of whites ensues.

1955

Emmett Till, a black teenager visiting in Mississippi, is found beaten to death, supposedly for making sexual advances to a young white storekeeper. His murderers are never sentenced. Only in 2017 does the storekeeper confess that her story, which incited the murder, was false.

On December 1, Rosa Parks is arrested for violating the bus segregation ordinance in Montgomery. Four days later the bus boycott begins in that city.

Martin Luther King's home is bombed.

A minister—an NAACP activist—is killed in Mississippi.

A law is passed in Mississippi to jail any white students who attend school with black students. Virginia defies school desegregation; Georgia defies park desegregation and threatens to fire any teachers supporting the *Brown* decision.

1955–1956

Autherine Lucy, a black woman, attempts to enroll in the University of Alabama as a graduate student. Following months of litigation, she is forced by the trustees to withdraw from campus, after mobs of whites riot on campus. The question of whether the mobs were students or laborers is raised in *Watchman*.

A rally of 15,000, the largest in the history of Montgomery, forms to celebrate Autherine Lucy's ouster. U.S. Senator James Eastland of Mississippi attends and speaks.

1956

On December 21, the bus boycott ends in Montgomery and buses are integrated. Ninety leaders are arrested. Alabama legislature asks for federal funds to deport black citizens to the North.

Nelle spends Christmas of this year with her friends, the dancer Joy Brown and her husband, Michael Brown, to whom she was introduced by Capote in 1947. They give her as a Christmas present enough money to take a year off to finish her manuscript. Shortly afterward she submits the *Watchman* manuscript to Maurice Crain, who agrees to serve as her agent.

Alabama outlaws the NAACP.

1957

Nelle completes *Watchman* and meets with Lippincott editors, one of whom is Tay Hohoff, and in October is offered a contract.

Willie Edwards is forced to jump from a bridge into the Alabama River.

Activist Ralph Abernathy's house is bombed.

An attempt is made to integrate the Little Rock, Arkansas, high school with nine black students.

1957–1959
Nelle works ceaselessly with Hohoff to revise her work, which is retitled and rewritten as *To Kill a Mockingbird*. In a letter, Capote asks one of his relatives about a rumor he has heard that Nelle is writing a book.

1958
Another church is bombed in Birmingham.

1959
A November 15 *New York Times* report of the murder of the Clutter family in Kansas gets Capote's attention. He asks Lee to go with him to Kansas to help him do research on the case. In December they travel to Garden City, Kansas. It becomes clear that much or most of the interviewing will have to be done by Nelle, given the residents' suspicion of Capote. They return at night to the Warren Hotel to type up the day's information. Nelle contributes 150 pages of her typed notes for the book. Capote, in a later (1966) interview with George Plimpton in the *New York Times Book Review*, enlarges on Lee's work on *In Cold Blood*. "She went on a number of interviews; she typed her own notes, . . . and I could refer to them. She was extremely helpful in the beginning, when we weren't making headway with the town's people, by making friends with the wives of the people I wanted to meet." When the call comes to the chief detective's house that suspects have been arrested, Lee and Capote are having dinner with his family. When they return to New York, the galleys of *To Kill a Mockingbird* are waiting for her.

1960
Except for the occasion of the executions of the two murderers, Lee would accompany Capote on every trip he made to Kansas—interviewing, writing, and offering encouragement. They are both present on March 22, the opening of the trial.

The official New York publication date planned for *Mockingbird* in July is delayed until fall because several book clubs select it—the Readers' Digest Condensed Books, a Book-of-the-Month Club alternate, and the British Book Society Choice. Several months before it hits the bookstores, it receives rave reviews, and she is overwhelmed with fan mail and requests for readings. Heinemann becomes her British publisher.

In this year anti-segregation sit-ins begin at a Greensboro, North Carolina, lunch counter.

1961
In May of this year, Freedom Riders leave DC for Alabama and other parts of the South, chiefly on buses, in the struggle for civil rights. Buses are attacked and

burned in Anniston, Alabama, where Freedom Riders are beaten and arrested. They are beaten by mobs in Montgomery and Birmingham.

A deal is closed for a film adaptation of *To Kill a Mockingbird* with Robert Mulligan (who plans to direct the film) and Alan Pakula (who will produce it). Horton Foote writes the screenplay after Lee turns down an offer to do it herself, and Gregory Peck is cast in the lead.

In April, Lee wins the Pulitzer Prize for literature. By this time the book has sold 500,000 copies. Lee writes an article for the April issue of *Vogue* entitled "Love—in Other Words," and the December issue of *McCall's* includes another Harper Lee article, "Christmas to Me," about what she insisted had to be a loan of money from Joy and Michael Brown.

Her sister Alice begins to handle Nelle's financial matters.

1962
On April 15 of this year, Amasa C. Lee dies.

Nelle continues to make trips to Kansas with Truman. She is present at all interviews he has with the defendants. Contrary to what the movie *Capote* suggests, Nelle insists that Truman was never successful in bribing his way into a cell.

Filming of *To Kill a Mockingbird* begins in February, and is wrapped up in June. The film premiers in Hollywood in December, and is nominated for eight Academy Awards and wins three.

In spring, members of the Southern Christian Leadership Conference, including thousands of children, march for civil rights in Birmingham, Alabama. Commissioner of Public Safety Bull Connor orders as many incarcerated as the jail will hold and then the protestors are attacked with high-pressure fire hoses and dogs. The actions continue for weeks until Attorney General Robert Kennedy intervenes. Nelle reports later that, on his return trip to New York, a photographer who visited her in Monroeville called her from Birmingham to report he had been roughed up and delayed in the bus station.

In September, James Meredith attempts to enter the University of Mississippi where violent mobs prompt the government to send in 5,000 troops. Two are killed.

Nelle begins a life devoted to reading, writing, golfing, visiting with friends like Joy Brown, playing cards, and attending classical music and dramatic events in the city. She regularly visits sister, Alice, in Monroeville but has no love for the town and is always eager to return to her home in New York.

1963
Medgar Evers, a leader in the NAACP, is murdered in Mississippi. Two hundred thousand protestors led by Martin Luther King march on Washington. Three young white and one young black civil rights workers are murdered in Mississippi. Four young girls are killed in a bombing of a Birmingham church.

1964

Marchers protesting segregated public restrooms and water fountains in Tusca-loosa, Alabama, are beaten and arrested.

The Civil Rights Act is passed.

1965

Selma marches for civil rights continue. One white woman protestor is shot and killed.

Capote attends the executions of the Clutter family murderers in Kansas. Both condemned men write their last letters to Nelle asking that she also be there, but it goes to the wrong address and does not reach her until it is over. By this time, both men have become disillusioned with Capote, believing that he cares more about his book than their lives. Capote sends the manuscript to Nelle to review. He fails to acknowledge Nelle's full part in writing *In Cold Blood* nor does he make any attempt to correct rumors that he had had a hand in writing *Mockingbird*.

1966

In Cold Blood is published, with a brief dedication to Capote's partner, Jack Dun-phy, and Harper Lee. In November, Capote hosts an enormous "Black and White Ball" at the Plaza Hotel with hundreds of his socialite friends. Nelle does not attend.

The Richmond, Virginia, school board decides to ban *Mockingbird* from the schools because it is "immoral literature." For various reasons, both on the left and right politically, it becomes one of the most banned books in modern history.

1968

Martin Luther King is shot and killed in Memphis, Tennessee.

Nelle's beloved agent, Maurice Crain, is found to have cancer and she spends much time helping take care of him.

Throughout the 1960s and 1970s Nelle is rumored to have been working on other books, which never materialize.

1970s

Tay Hohoff retires from Lippincott and Crain dies. By the late 1970s, *Mockingbird* has reportedly sold 10 million copies.

The relationship between Lee and Capote falls completely apart—a result, not only of the *In Cold Blood* disappointment, but his abuse of alcohol and drugs, and, according to Nelle, his inexcusable treatment of his long-time lover.

1978

Nelle goes to Alexander City, Alabama, at the request of a victim's family to inves-tigate an unsolved serial murder. She takes up the project and works on it through-out the 1980s. Lippincott is bought by Harper & Row, later HarperCollins.

1984

Truman Capote dies and Nelle attends his funeral.

1988

In a biography of Capote, the statement is made that Nelle's mother tried to drown her, a charge that Nelle and Alice vehemently deny.

1990s

To Nelle's extreme dissatisfaction, Monroeville begins to capitalize on the extraordinary success of *To Kill a Mockingbird*. Murals are painted on buildings, a statue of Atticus is erected, plays of the novel are produced, and a museum is opened, selling such things as *The Recipes of Calpurnia*.

1995

A 35th anniversary edition of *Mockingbird* is issued. In the interview, Nelle says she had abandoned the Alexander City project when someone called and proposed to "sell" his grandmother to her as an informant.

1999

A *Library Journal* poll names *To Kill a Mockingbird* the best novel of the century.

2001

Nelle is interviewed by Marja Mills of the *Chicago Tribune*.

2004

At the request of Kansas law enforcement, Nelle visits the special collections on *In Cold Blood* in the New York Public Library to see if she can find evidence that Capote never visited the defendants' cells in the prison, as is to be portrayed in the film *Capote*.

With Nelle's encouragement, Mills rents the house next door to Alice's where she lives for two years while writing a book on the experience of living next to Alice.

2005

Nelle is portrayed by Catherine Keener in the film *Capote*, about their experiences in Kansas. Nelle highly praised Philip Seymour Hoffman's performance but cites numerous serious inaccuracies in the story.

2006

Nelle is played by Sandra Bullock in *Infamous*, another Capote-centered film.

2007

Nelle suffers a severe stroke. After short hospitalizations in New York City and Birmingham, Alabama, she moves to Meadows Assisted Living facility in Monroeville, the home of her sister Alice.

She is awarded the Presidential Medal of Freedom by George Bush in November.

2010

Nelle wins the National Medal of the Arts.

2011

A copy of the manuscript *Go Set a Watchman* is discovered by two of Nelle's literary advisors while her lawyer Tonja Carter is present.

In December Alice breaks ribs, gets pneumonia, and moves to Englewood Nursing Home.

2013

Nelle sues her *Mockingbird* agent over theft of her royalties. Her legal team also sues the Monroeville museum.

2014

Lawyer Carter "rediscovers" the manuscript and sends it to Lee's agent, Andrew Nurnberg. Nelle's nephew, however, remembers reading *Watchman* even before the publication of *Mockingbird*.

Nelle's sister Alice dies on November 17.

Marja Mills publishes *The Mockingbird Next Door: Life with Harper Lee.*

2015

Several months after Alice's death, in February, the announcement of the forthcoming publication of *Watchman* creates considerable controversy, considering Nelle's earlier wishes to avoid further publication and publicity and her present state of mind, in short, whether Nelle actually could or did approve publication. *Go Set a Watchman* is released in July to mixed reviews and concerns over its portrayal of Atticus. Many who loved *Mockingbird* refuse to read the new novel.

2016

On February 19, seven months after the publication of *Go Set a Watchman*, Nelle Harper Lee dies.

Notes on Sources

Bibliographic information for works discussed in Notes on Sources appears in the Further Reading sections at the ends of the relevant chapters.

Life

The last book-length biography of Nelle Harper Lee is Charles Shields's *Mockingbird: A Portrait of Harper Lee*. Although Lee vigorously objected to the biography and it has its flaws, for the most part it is a well researched project that is useful for its chronology of events, especially in Lee's pre–New York years. As Shields has suspected, most of Lee's displeasure may have arisen from his conclusions about her ancestors, comments about her mother, his assumption in the introduction that because she never married, she may well have been a lesbian, and the myth that because she avoided the press, she was a secluded loner. Although I implored her to finish the book and make notations of inaccuracies, she said she was just unable to read the whole thing.

My narrative of her university years was supplemented by my unpublished interviews with her in person and on the telephone, as well as conversations with my colleague in the University of Alabama English Department James McMillan, one of her closest Tuscaloosa friends. Both sources confirmed her unhappiness with her education there.

Joy Brown provided details of Lee's early life in New York City and her early publishing efforts. I also prevailed upon her to double-check my chronology with regard to events in Nelle's life.

Works on Truman Capote and *In Cold Blood* are valuable sources for Lee's relationship with Capote and, especially, their work together in Kansas. See Gerald Clarke's biography, *Capote*; the recent book by Ralph Voss, *Truman Capote and the Legacy of "In Cold Blood"*; and Capote's own fiction, *Other Voices, Other Rooms*. The accounts given in these sources were augmented by my own telephone conversations with Nelle Harper after the movie *Capote* appeared in 2005.

Casey Cep, in the *New Yorker*, and Kim Chandler, in the *Huffington Post*, have done exhaustive research on Lee's last abortive project: investigation of serial murders in Alexander City, Alabama. Cep has taken up the project and published a book on it: *Furious Hours: Harper Lee and an Unfinished Story of Race, Religion, and Murder* (forthcoming).

Marja Mills's *The Mockingbird Next Door*, about her two-year residence in Monroeville, as well as my conversations with Mills, throw light on the life and mind of Nelle Harper in her last years in New York City, then in Monroeville. Despite Lee's signed objection, obtained by her lawyer, her sister Alice confirmed their support for the project and wrote that Nelle, at that later point of declining health, would sign anything put before her.

The details of the controversial last year of Nelle Harper's life and the publication of *Go Set a Watchman* are richly laid out in multiple articles in the top newspapers in the United States and England. See especially Alexandra Alter, William Grimes, Michiko Kakutani, and Serge Kovaleski of the *New York Times*; Ron Charles of the *Washington Post*; and Philip Hensler of *The Telegraph*.

Historical Context

The most useful general histories of the period are Howard Zinn's *A People's History of the United States* and T. H. Watkins's *The Great Depression: America in the 1930s*. Two classic histories specific to the pre–civil-rights-era race relations in the South of *To Kill a Mockingbird* are Clarence Cason's *90° in the Shade* and W. J. Cash's *The Mind of the South*. Carrying the history forward is Joel Williamson's *A Rage for Order: Black/White Relations in the American South since Emancipation*.

Further information on the period comes from my unpublished interviews with Oscar Berland and Jim McWilliams.

One of the most iconic books on the Scottsboro Boys is Dan T. Carter's *Scottsboro: A Tragedy of the American South*, in which he considers the details of the arrests, what lay behind the charges, the everyday (almost minute-by-minute) workings of the court, the truthful and the lying witnesses, the responses of people in general within the state, the quarrels between different defense groups, and the fate of the defendants. Here are made plain the connections we find between Scottsboro and Maycomb: the charges, the moral character, shortcomings, and fear of the white women involved that elicited both outrage and sympathy, the limitations of the jury and jury system, the guilty verdicts despite evidence to the contrary, and the words of Judge Horton, so rhetorically similar to those of Atticus.

The following are works specific to historical topics raised by *To Kill a Mockingbird* and *Go Set a Watchman*.

The Ku Klux Klan: Wayne Greenhaw, *Fighting the Devil in Dixie: How Civil Rights Activists Took On the Ku Klux Klan in Alabama*

Lynching: The Alabama Department of Archives and History at Tuskegee Institute

Labor: Robin Kelley, *Hammer and Hoe: Alabama Communists during the Great Depression*

The White Citizens' Council: Neil R. McMillen, *The Citizens' Council: Organized Resistance to the Second Reconstruction, 1954–64*

NAACP: Charles Flint Kellogg, *NAACP: A History of the National Association for the Advancement of Colored People*

Brown v. Board of Education: Richard Kluger, *Simple Justice: The History of Brown v. Board of Education and Black America's Struggle for Equality*

Montgomery Bus Boycott: David Aretha, *Montgomery Bus Boycott*

Autherine Lucy: Culpepper Clark, *The Schoolhouse Door: Segregation's Last Stand at the University of Alabama*

Literary Analysis

For all its impact and influence, little attention has been given to critical analysis of *To Kill a Mockingbird*. Claudia Durst Johnson's *To Kill a Mockingbird: Threatening Boundaries* and *Understanding "To Kill a Mockingbird"* first established the importance of the gothic, gothic parody, and the Scottsboro Boys trials to a reading of the novel. William Patrick Day's *In the Circles of Fear and Desire: A Study of Gothic Fantasy* is essential background to a literary study of *To Kill a Mockingbird*. Several collections of essays on *To Kill a Mockingbird* are valuable: *"To Kill a Mockingbird": Modern Critical Interpretations*, edited by Harold Bloom; a collection of articles in the *Alabama Law Review* in the winter of 1994; and *Readings on "To Kill a Mockingbird*," edited by Terry O'Neill. Also see R. A. Dave's analysis in *Indian Studies in American Fiction*.

Reviews of *Go Set a Watchman* appeared shortly after that novel's recent publication. Some useful ones include Mark Lawson's review in *The Guardian*, Julia Keller's in the *Chicago Tribune*, and Randall Kennedy's and Michiko Kakutani's in the *New York Times*.

Race Relations in the Two Novels

See the list of further reading for chapter 4 for material on race in *To Kill a Mockingbird* and *Go Set a Watchman*. Especially useful are the following on topics (mentioned specifically in the two novels) relevant to race: Culpepper Clark, Charles Flint Kellogg, Richard Kluger, Neil McMillen, Timothy Tyson, Wyn Craig Wade, and Joel Williamson.

Women's Issues

The behavior expected of proper little girls and young ladies can be found in works by Jenny Bradley, Meg Foster, and Brett Harvey. Personal memoirs—by Claire Steer Fortune and Anne Wardell—bear out the expected attire of little girls like Scout.

See Lewine Mair for women's limited place on the golf course.

"Women's Role in the 1950s" in *American Decades* illuminates the world in which Jean Louise finds herself in Maycomb.

A fresh perspective on gender and a tomboy like Scout is offered in a *New York Times* op-ed piece by Lisa Selin Davis: "Girls Can Still Be Tomboys."

Social Class

Allison Davis, Burleigh B. Gardner, and Mary R. Gardner have written one sociological book on class structure in general and one anthropological study of the Deep South. Other studies of class in the Deep South, most of them pertinent to *To Kill a Mockingbird*, are by W. J. Cash, Clarence Cason, Virginia Van der Veer Hamilton, and George Brown Tindall.

Several books focus on the lower classes. Two general studies of class, covering all of the United States, one by Sheldon Hackney and one by Nancy Isenberg, are pertinent to *Go Set a Watchman*.

Carl Grafton and Anne Permaloff's *Big Mules and Branchheads* and Wayne Flynt's *Poor but Proud* are excellent books on the working classes in Alabama. Both provide background useful in the study of both novels.

One of the few works that studies class in *To Kill a Mockingbird* is Teresa Godwin Phelps's *Alabama Law Review* article, "The Margins of Maycomb: A Rereading of *To Kill a Mockingbird*."

The South

The culture of the Old South, a heritage that continued to be strong well into the 20th century (and for the characters in Harper Lee's novels), has been explored in three studies that focus their attention on the influence of "Sir Walter Scott" romance: Carl Carmer's *Stars Fell on Alabama*, W. J. Cash's *The Mind of the South*, and Clarence Cason's *90° in the Shade*, all distinguished studies of the distinctive Southern character. The gothic style is also apparent in the fiction of William Faulkner. His short story "A Rose for Emily" depicts the psychological destructiveness caused by the lingering sick romance of the region.

A more recent useful study is Bertram Wyatt-Brown's *The Shaping of Southern Culture: Honor, Grace, and War*.

James C. Cobb's *The Selling of the South: The Southern Crusade for Industrial Development* looks at the characteristics we see developed in Henry Clinton and the other men of the "New Alabama" of *Go Set a Watchman*.

The Hero

A theoretical book on heroes in general is Scott T. Allison and George R. Goethal's *Heroes: What They Do and Why We Need Them*.

Two of the first writers to question the heroism of Atticus in *To Kill a Mockingbird* were Monroe Freedman in 1992: "Atticus Finch, Esq., R.I.P.: A Gentleman but No Model for a Lawyer"; and Teresa Godwin Phelps in 1994: "The Margins of Maycomb: A Rereading of *To Kill a Mockingbird*." These two were unusual perspectives before the publication of *Go Set a Watchman*.

Most of the documents pondering the fall of the hero, Atticus, appeared after the publication of *Go Set a Watchman*. These include articles in 2015 in the *New York Times* by Alexandra Alter, Michiko Kakutani, and Serge Kovaleski; and in *The Telegraph* by Jane Shilling; and in 2016 in *The Atlantic* by Megan Garber.

Censorship

Any general work on censorship in the United States will include mention of *To Kill a Mockingbird*. A book devoted entirely to censorship is *100 Banned Books*, edited by Nicholas J. Karolides, Margaret Bald, and Dawn B. Sova. It includes a section on Harper Lee's novel. An essay by Jill May in *Censored Books: Critical Viewpoints* covers *To Kill a Mockingbird*. The reader also has available a letter on censorship of the novel written by the author herself in 1966. It appeared in the *Richmond News Leader*.

Regarding *Go Set a Watchman*, Jane Shilling is one of many people who decided *not* to read the recently published novel—what I have labeled here as "self-censorship."

Relevance Today

Some of the many articles on the shooting of black men were written by Larry Buchanan ("What Happened in Ferguson"); Eric Heisig ("Tamir Rice Shooting"); Mitch Smith ("Officer Cleared"); and Lucia Walinches ("Tulsa Officer Cites Her Training").

Three recent articles by Adam Liptak and two books discuss the continuing problem of gerrymandering. The books are Gloria J. Browne Marshall's *The Voting Rights War* and Anthony J. McCann and Charles Anthony Smith's *Gerrymandering in America*. These works speak to the problem of thwarting the minority vote.

A comprehensive account of the massacre in Charleston, South Carolina, is Edward Ball's "United States v. Dylann Roof." This includes Roof's actions during the day before the evening's shooting.

An editorial in the *New York Times*, "A Protest with Echoes of the Klan," sums up the white supremacists' responses to attempts to take down Confederate flags and statues throughout the South. Also see Eric Foner on the history of Confederate statues and the front-page *New York Times* article on the Charlottesville violence by Sheryl Gay Stolberg and Brian M. Rosenthal.

On the subject of women, see three works: Jennifer Rand's *Huffington Post* article on the "third wave"; and books by Rebecca Traister and Sheryl Sandberg, all of whom researched changes in women's lives in the 21st century.

For a study of the strong woman in popular culture, see Kelly Lawler, "Spoilers: Five Wonderfully Feminist Moments in 'Wonder Woman.'"

On current heroism, see the balanced view by Sharon Otterman and Matthew Wald in the *New York Times* and Andy Pasztor in the *Wall Street Journal* of Chesley Sullenberger's heroism and the investigation into his decision to land his plane in the water rather than trying to return to the airport.

The fall of Bill Cosby, who was known for years as "the American father," is reported by Eugene Robinson in the *Washington Post*: "Cosby and the Crumbling of a True Pop Culture Icon."

Index

About the Author

Claudia Durst Johnson, PhD, is a writer and retired professor from the University of Alabama. Her books include *To Kill a Mockingbird: Threatening Boundaries*, *Understanding To Kill a Mockingbird*, and numerous other works on subjects such as Nathaniel Hawthorne, daily life in colonial America, and American theater. She won a *Choice* Award for her book *American Actress: Perspective on the Nineteenth Century*.